W9-AXP-446

✧ *Companions for the Journey* ✧

Praying with Francis de Sales

by
Thomas F. Dailey, OSFS

Saint Mary's Press
Christian Brothers Publications
Winona, Minnesota

Genuine recycled paper with 10% post-consumer waste.
Printed with soy-based ink.

The words of Francis de Sales are collected in twenty-seven volumes of the *Oeuvres de Saint François de Sales, Evêque de Genève et Docteur de l'Eglise, Edition Complète, d'après les autographes et les éditions originales . . . publiée . . . par les soins des Religieuses de la Visitation du Premier Monastère* (Annecy: J. Niérat, 1892–1964). Wherever possible, quotations are taken from existing English translations. Otherwise, the citation *OEA* with volume and page numbers refers to the collected edition of the original.

The publishing team for this book included Carl Koch, series editor; Rosemary Broughton, development editor; Laurie A. Berg, copy editor; Lynn Dahdal, production editor; Holly Storkel, typesetter; Elaine Kohner, illustrator; Kent Linder, cover designer; Maurine R. Twait, art director; pre-press, printing, and binding by the graphics division of Saint Mary's Press.

Printed in the United States of America

Printing: 9 8 7 6 5 4 3 2 1

Year: 2005 04 03 02 01 00 99 98 97

ISBN 0-88489-495-9

✧ Contents ✧

✧ Foreword ✧

Companions for the Journey

Just as food is required for human life, so are companions. Indeed, the word *companions* comes from two Latin words: *com,* meaning "with," and *panis,* meaning "bread." Companions nourish our heart, mind, soul, and body. They are also the people with whom we can celebrate the sharing of bread.

Perhaps the most touching stories in the Bible are about companionship: the Last Supper, the wedding feast at Cana, the sharing of the loaves and the fishes, and Jesus' breaking of bread with the disciples on the road to Emmaus. Each incident of companionship with Jesus revealed more about his mercy, love, wisdom, suffering, and hope. When Jesus went to pray in the Garden of Olives, he craved the companionship of the Apostles. They let him down. But God sent the Spirit to inflame the hearts of the Apostles, and they became faithful companions to Jesus and to one another.

Throughout history, other faithful companions have followed Jesus and the Apostles. These saints and mystics have also taken the journey from conversion, through suffering, to resurrection. Just as they were inspired by the holy people who went before them, so too may you be inspired by these saints and mystics and take them as your companions on your spiritual journey.

The Companions for the Journey series is a response to the spiritual hunger of Christians. This series makes available the rich spiritual teachings of mystics and guides whose wisdom can help us on our pilgrimage. As you complete the last meditation in each volume, it is hoped that you will feel supported, challenged, and affirmed by a soul-companion on your spiritual journey.

The spiritual hunger that has emerged over the last twenty years is a great sign of renewal in Christian life. People fill retreat programs and workshops on topics in spirituality. The demand for spiritual directors exceeds the number available. Interest in the lives and writings of saints and mystics is increasing as people search for models of whole and holy Christian life.

Praying with Francis

Praying with Francis de Sales is more than just a book about Francis's spirituality. This book seeks to engage you in praying in the way that Francis did about issues and themes that were central to his experience. Each meditation can enlighten your understanding of his spirituality and lead you to reflect on your own experience.

The goal of *Praying with Francis de Sales* is that you will discover Francis's rich spirituality and integrate his spirit and wisdom into your relationship with God, with your brothers and sisters, and with your own heart and mind.

Suggestions for Praying with Francis

Meet Francis de Sales, a fascinating companion for your pilgrimage, by reading the introduction to this book. It provides a brief biography of Francis and an outline of the major themes of his spirituality.

Once you meet Francis de Sales, you will be ready to pray with him and to encounter God, your sisters and brothers, and yourself in new and wonderful ways. To help your prayer, here are some suggestions that have been part of the tradition of Christian spirituality:

Create a sacred space. Jesus said, "'Whenever you pray, go into your room and shut the door and pray to your [God] who is in secret; and your [God] who sees in secret will reward you'" (Matthew 6:6). Solitary prayer is best done in a place where you can have privacy and silence, both of which can be luxuries in the life of busy people. If privacy and silence are not possible, create a quiet, safe place within yourself, perhaps while riding to and from work, while sitting in line at the dentist's office, or while waiting for someone. Do the best you can, knowing that a loving God is present everywhere. Whether the meditations in this book are used for solitary prayer or with a group, try to create a prayerful mood with candles, meditative music, an open Bible, or a crucifix.

Open yourself to the power of prayer. Every human experience has a religious dimension. All of life is suffused with God's presence. So remind yourself that God is present as you begin your period of prayer. Do not worry about distractions. If something keeps intruding during your prayer, spend some time talking with God about it. Be flexible because God's spirit blows where it will.

Prayer can open your mind and widen your vision. Be open to new ways of seeing God, people, and yourself. As you open yourself to the spirit of God, different emotions are evoked, such as sadness from tender memories, or joy from a celebration recalled. Our emotions are messages from God that can tell us much about our spiritual quest. Also, prayer strengthens our will to act. Through prayer, God can touch our will and empower us to live according to what we know is true.

Finally, many of the meditations in this book will call you to employ your memories, your imagination, and the circumstances of your life as subjects for prayer. The great mystics and saints realized that they had to use all their resources to know God better. Indeed, God speaks to us continually and touches us constantly. We must learn to listen and feel with all the means that God has given us.

Come to prayer with an open mind, heart, and will.

Preview each meditation before beginning. After you have placed yourself in God's presence, spend a few moments previewing the readings and especially the reflection activities. Several reflection activities are given in each meditation because different styles of prayer appeal to different personalities or personal needs. **Note that each meditation has more**

reflection activities than can be done during one prayer period. Therefore, select only one or two reflection activities each time you use a meditation. Do not feel compelled to complete all the reflection activities.

Read meditatively. Each meditation offers you a story about Francis and a reading from his writings. Take your time reading. If a particular phrase touches you, stay with it. Relish its feelings, meanings, and concerns.

Use the reflections. Following the readings is a short reflection in commentary form, which is meant to give perspective to the readings. Then you are offered several ways of meditating on the readings and the theme of the prayer. You may be familiar with the different methods of meditating, but in case you are not, they are described briefly here:

✦ *Repeated short prayer or mantra:* One means of focusing your prayer is to use a *mantra,* or "prayer word." The mantra may be a single word or a short phrase taken from the readings or from the Scriptures. For example, a short prayer for meditation 1 in this book might simply be "heart speaks to heart." Repeated slowly in harmony with your breathing, the mantra helps you center your heart and mind on one action or attribute of God.

✦ *Lectio divina:* This type of meditation is "divine studying," a concentrated reflection on the word of God or the wisdom of a spiritual writer. Most often in *lectio divina,* you will be invited to read one of the passages several times and then concentrate on one or two sentences, pondering their meaning for you and their effect on you. *Lectio divina* commonly ends with formulation of a resolution.

✦ *Guided meditation:* In this type of meditation, our imagination helps us consider alternative actions and likely consequences. Our imagination helps us experience new ways of seeing God, our neighbors, ourselves, and nature. When Jesus told his followers parables and stories, he engaged their imagination. In this book, you will be invited to follow guided meditations.

One way of doing a guided meditation is to read the scene or story several times, until you know the outline and can recall it when you enter into reflection. Or before your prayer time, you may wish to record the meditation on a tape recorder. If so, remember to allow pauses for reflection between phrases and to speak with a slow, peaceful pace and tone. Then, during prayer, when you have finished the readings and the reflection commentary, you can turn on your recording of the meditation and be led through it. If you find your own voice too distracting, ask a friend to make the tape for you.

✦ *Examen of consciousness:* The reflections often will ask you to examine how God has been speaking to you in your past and present experience—in other words, the reflections will ask you to examine your awareness of God's presence in your life.

✦ *Journal writing:* Writing is a process of discovery. If you write for any length of time, stating honestly what is on your mind and in your heart, you will unearth much about who you are, how you stand with your God, what deep longings reside in your soul, and more. In some reflections, you will be asked to write a dialog with Jesus or someone else. If you have never used writing as a means of meditation, try it. Reserve a special notebook for your journal writing. If desired, you can go back to your entries at a future time for an examen of consciousness.

✦ *Action:* Occasionally, a reflection will suggest singing a favorite hymn, going out for a walk, or undertaking some other physical activity. Actions can be meaningful forms of prayer.

Using the Meditations for Group Prayer

If you wish to use the meditations for community prayer, these suggestions may help:

✦ Read the theme to the group. Call the community into the presence of God, using the short opening prayer. Invite one or two participants to read one or both readings. If you use both readings, observe the pause between them.

+ The reflection commentary may be used as a reading, or it can be deleted, depending on the needs and interests of the group.
+ Select one of the reflection activities for your group. Allow sufficient time for your group to reflect, to recite a centering prayer or mantra, to accomplish a studying prayer (*lectio divina*), or to finish an examen of consciousness. Depending on the group and the amount of available time, you may want to invite the participants to share their reflections, responses, or petitions with the group.
+ Reading the passage from the Scriptures may serve as a summary of the meditation.
+ If a formulated prayer or a psalm is given as a closing, it may be recited by the entire group. Or you may ask participants to offer their own prayers for the closing.

Now you are ready to begin praying with Francis de Sales, a faithful and caring companion on this stage of your spiritual journey. It is hoped that you will find him to be a true soul-companion.

CARL KOCH
Editor

✧ Introduction ✧

Reborn Through the Love of God

In the book *A World Waiting to Be Born,* the popular psychologist M. Scott Peck claims in his opening chapter that "Something Is Seriously Wrong" with our modern world. That something, he argues, is the ever growing phenomenon of incivility, or being hurtful to others. In this day and age where the concern for oneself above all others breeds an infectious materialism and a callous disregard for life, the practice of a true civility—the awareness of and intention of being genuinely good to others—is surely lacking, both in our interpersonal relationships and in our societal institutions.

Four centuries ago another popular writer, Francis de Sales (1567–1622), envisioned a world already reborn through the love of God. Francis's vision of this world was founded on a deep appreciation of the love that God has showered upon us through the gifts of creation and human life, particularly in the life, death, and Resurrection of Jesus Christ. Francis believed that beauty and goodness are the hallmarks of our world, as gifts born from God's deep and abiding love for each of us. Enabled and ennobled by this love, we are capable of much more than we might imagine. We are capable of living a true life of devotion in this world. We are capable of giving birth to a new world.

Francis's spirit has permeated the Christian world. His life story, his written treasury, and his religious legacy—all point to the virtuous qualities of a man imbued with the love of God and desirous of sharing that love with all who would seek it. Francis remains today a spiritual patron for the following people:

✦ those who seek union with God in the midst of the affairs
of this world
✦ those who struggle to lead a life of virtue amidst the temptations of this world
✦ those who desire to grow in prayerful awareness of the
presence of God in the world

Known affectionately as the "gentleman saint," Francis models for us a type of civility that has God as its origin and its
goal. Indeed, his spirit of practical holiness fills the pages of
his life's story.

Francis's Story

In the papal decree by which Francis was named a Doctor of
the Church, Pope Pius IX praised the saint "not only for the
sublime holiness of life which he achieved, but also for the
wisdom with which he directed souls in the way of sanctity"
(*Rerum omnium perturbationem*, 4). Though renowned for his
many accomplishments in a relatively short life, Francis remains an attractive companion for the spiritual journey due to
his profoundly simple approach to the divine events of everyday life.

A Humanistic Education

Francis was born in 1567, at a time when the great flowering
of the Renaissance blossomed throughout Europe. Growing
up in the environs of Savoy (in the region that is now south-
eastern France and western Switzerland), he was surrounded
by the beauty of nature, from the majestic Alps to the serene
Lake of Geneva. In such surroundings he could not help but
be stirred to soulful wonder at the goodness present in all of
creation through the beneficence of the Creator.

As the eldest of thirteen children raised in a family of nobility, Francis was educated in the finest traditions of human-
ism and the liberal arts. At the Collège de La Roche-sur-Foron,
the six-year-old Francis was tutored by Father Déage to bear
the qualities of "docility, facility in learning, [and] piety" (An-

dré Ravier, *Francis de Sales: Sage and Saint,* p. 20). Three years later, at the Chappuisien College in Annecy, he began his formal studies, with an emphasis on learning French language and literature. Having received the sacraments of Communion and Confirmation during this time, Francis also began his lifelong devotion to the church. That devotion was soon to be tested during his studies at Clermont College, a Jesuit school in Paris, where he was sent in 1578. There he pursued the "arts" of education (the classics, humanities, rhetoric, etc.) and of nobility (horsemanship, fencing, dancing, etc.), learning all that was expected of a young gentleman. But he also undertook, on his own, the study of theology.

In 1586, after listening to the learned debates at the Sorbonne on the notion of predestination, Francis found himself mired in a personal crisis in which he feared that he would be eternally damned. Then and there he resolved to serve God completely throughout the whole of his life. For a young man of nineteen years of age, this event was to become the defining moment in his life, one that would color his optimistic vision of the world and influence the hope-filled character of his writings.

After a brief return to his native Savoy, Francis continued his studies at the University of Padua. There, in 1592, he earned doctoral degrees in both civil and canon law. There, too, he continued his independent study of theology under the direction of Antonio Possevino, a famous Jesuit. At this time Francis composed the "Spiritual Exercises," a rule of life for himself that he would later modify for his spiritual children. With such an extraordinary education, he was soon admitted to the bar and named a senator, steps along the way to his father's dream of a successful diplomatic career for Francis. But the providential God had other plans for this young nobleman.

What characterizes the education of this saint might well be described as a natural goodness. Inspired by the beauty of the land around him, Francis came to realize that the world is essentially good, that all things participate in the beauty and goodness of the Creator, and that human life itself is ordered to this beauty and goodness of God as its ultimate end. In our world today, scientific discoveries and technological break-throughs reflect the potential of creation. Yet, at the same time, these powerful advances run the risk of fragmenting our life. The holistic and humanistic education that Francis received and would later promote serves to remind us of the overarching plan of salvation that God has in store for our world as it waits to be reborn.

The Priest-Missionary

Declining the opportunities arranged by his father to become a powerful diplomat, Francis was named provost of the cathedral chapter of Geneva and ordained to the priesthood at age twenty-six. His first assignment was to restore Catholicism to the region of the Chablais (in modern Switzerland).

The duchy of Savoy suffered the ravages of political wars, among them an invasion by the king of France in 1536, and later battles to return the land to the duke (during the years 1589–1598). In religious terms, though, the region of the Chablais was the land of Calvinism. With the advent of the Reformation there, the Catholic bishop of Geneva had been exiled to nearby Annecy. Now, with Geneva as its leading city and Theodore de Beze as Calvin's successor, the populace of that territory was decidedly antipapist. "Of the some twenty-five thousand souls who inhabited the area, only about a hundred Catholics remained. All the others passed—either by choice or by force—into Protestantism" (Ravier, *Sage and Saint*, p. 62).

Amid the political-religious hostilities of this environment, Francis undertook the personally challenging effort to reach out to the common people. Journeying at risk of life and limb, and celebrating the Mass despite public indifference or hostility, he established contacts with the people by writing little pamphlets and placing them under doors or on streetposts. In this way, little by little, he initiated open discussions about the truths of religion. Two more works, apologetic in nature, would flow from his pen at this time: *Catholic Controversy* and *Defense of the Standard of the Holy Cross*.

Engaging the citizens of the land on their own terms, he slowly but assuredly led them to a reconsideration of their beliefs. Eventually, after continued writing and prominent debates with the Calvinist leaders, Francis was able to convert the majority of the inhabitants of that region. Commemorating this missionary success, both the duke of Savoy and the legate of Pope Clement VIII (Cardinal de Medici) recognized the extraordinary "'dedication to the Catholic Faith and . . . zeal for the salvation of souls'" which the young priest demonstrated (Ravier, *Sage and Saint,* p. 85). That dedication and zeal would soon spread far and wide.

Perhaps the secret of his missionary success came from Francis's sincere efforts to dialog with everyone. In the midst of conflict and danger, his peaceful pursuit of the truth elicited from one and all a profound respect and a sympathetic hearing. In a world today where religion and politics often form a combustible combination, a similar search for truth may help combat the prevailing mind-set of a pluralism that values only an "openness" to all ideas, regardless of their validity. And, in our contemporary pursuit of religious and social unity, the respect for the goodness of the other person, championed by the young priest, serves to remind us of what is essential in our common life.

The Bishop of Geneva

Having completed his work in the Chablais, Francis returned to Annecy, where he was soon appointed coadjutor bishop. Four years later, in 1602, he was consecrated Bishop of Geneva. At this time the church was in the process of appropriating the teachings of the Council of Trent in response to the Protestant Reformation.

The new bishop took it upon himself to educate his diocese in the doctrines of the church. As the prominent religious figure in the region, Francis preached often and his sermons became known for their manifold eloquence. Yet, he endeavored to foster the faith beyond the confines of the church buildings. He organized diocesan synods and initiated the practice of parish visitations. He also formed a Confraternity of Christian Doctrine and personally taught the catechism classes. His zeal for imparting knowledge was such that he even invented a type of sign language by which he taught a young man who was born deaf. Later, he cofounded the Florimontane Academy, a precursor to today's French Academy, where humanistic scholars of all interests could engage in discussion.

Francis's achievements garnered national recognition, and he was invited to preach and teach throughout France. Though he declined an offer to become archbishop of Paris, his travels led him to encounters with Jane de Chantal, Vincent de Paul, and others who would later play significant roles in the promotion of the spiritual life.

In his pastoral work as shepherd of the diocese, Francis put into practice what may seem to many a commonplace idea. He emphasized a direct and personal contact with the people in his care, commoner and scholar alike. In today's world affairs, where levels of bureaucracy can be daunting and discouraging, the administrative example of the bishop of Geneva serves to remind us that our faith is not simply an academic exercise or merely an institutional affiliation. Rather, to give birth to the world of God's love, faith is to be lived in the midst of the world, in the concrete and everyday life of people in the world. There Francis was right at home. There Francis invites us to dwell.

The Spiritual Director

The religious reformation that took place during Francis's time brought with it a confusion over the truths of religion. People of all walks of life were searching for some direction. Due to his many contacts with people in his diocese and beyond, Francis was ardently sought after for spiritual counsel.

He responded to these spiritual seekers in a simple yet impressive way. Francis wrote letters—thousands of letters! Because of his hectic schedule as spiritual leader of the diocese, he would often have to steal time in the morning or before bed to reply to the many queries that the faithful would pose. It is estimated that he wrote over ten thousand such letters, but most have been destroyed. From the letters that are preserved, we get a glimpse of the profound simplicity of this spiritual director. Whether writing to members of religious orders, well-to-do nobles, or even simple laborers, Francis faithfully gave instructions on a wide variety of issues affecting the daily life of believers, from raising children to fulfilling duties and dealing with death. It was precisely in the midst of these otherwise mundane affairs that Francis taught his spiritual children to find God. Ever humble and always encouraging, his letters of spiritual direction endeared him to all who sought his wisdom.

One of those with whom Francis shared spiritual advice deserves particular mention—Jane de Chantal. A young widow with four children, Jane met Francis when he was preaching the Lenten sermons in Dijon in 1604. Inspired by this holy man, a man manifestly inspired with a divine vision, Jane eventually convinced Francis to become her spiritual director. Through written correspondence and by means of personal encounters whenever their travels would permit, Francis and Jane entered into a spiritual friendship that would blossom and bear fruit in the living legacy now known as Salesian spirituality.

What his letters of spiritual direction reveal is Francis's "inspired common sense" (*Selected Letters*, pp. 33–34) and his keen awareness of the practical dimension to holiness. Always drawing on the positive, he taught people to find God wherever they were and to love God in whatever they were doing. Along the way, Francis exemplified the virtues of true spiritual friendship, building relationships that had as their foundation and focus the common desire to love God more and more. In a world where interpersonal relationships so often are superficial or directed only to self-serving aims, Francis's advice and example demonstrate for us the value of relationships centered on divine love.

The Devotional Writer

From his informal letters, Francis quickly gained a reputation as a masterful communicator of things spiritual. His popularity was such that the recipients of these letters cajoled him to publish lengthier works on the subject of Christian life in the world. Among his many writings, two spiritual classics deserve particular mention.

The first, *Introduction to the Devout Life,* was published in 1609, and was the forerunner of what the Second Vatican Council would later teach as the universal call to holiness. This book, addressed to the fictional "Philothea" (a soul loving or in love with God), proposes a simple yet at that time revolutionary idea, namely, that devotion is possible in every state and condition of life. Francis wrote in the preface:

> My purpose is to instruct those who live in town, within families, or at court, and by their state of life are obliged to live an ordinary life as to outward appearances. . . . I shall show to such [persons] that . . . a strong, resolute soul can live in the world without being infected by any of its moods, find sweet springs of piety amid its salty waves, and fly through the flames of earthly lusts without burning the wings of its holy desires for a devout life. (Pp. 33–34)

Francis constructed this spiritual primer on the edifice of the Ignatian exercises he was familiar with from his Jesuit education. Following upon a series of meditations designed to bring one to embrace the resolution to lead a devout life, Francis then expounds upon this life with his personal instructions concerning prayer and the sacraments, the practice of virtue, the struggle against temptations, and the renewal of one's life.

The second work, his *Treatise on the Love of God,* was published in 1616, and is a more far-reaching attempt at analyzing the workings of divine love in human life. Supported by a sound philosophy and psychology of the human person, and annotated with explanations from the Bible and examples from the world of nature, this treatise seeks to spell out in detail the quest for the soul's union with the will of God, as learned through meditation and contemplation. Though not as widely circulated as the *Introduction,* this book, together with Francis's many other writings, constitutes a written legacy that can be trusted to lead readers surely and certainly along the way to God.

The popularity of Francis's writing may be attributed to two factors. On the one hand, his instructions on the devout life are filled with great spiritual imagination. Acknowledged as a literary genius in his own right, Francis is able to paint

meaning with words and to convey truth through metaphoric language. On the other hand, this imaginative power is clearly directed to a practical end. His writings address the common needs of everyday people, and he teaches them that the profound mysteries of God's love can be appropriated in the virtues of everyday living. In a world today that is inundated with questionable messages carried by film and television, the imaginative writings of Francis de Sales offer a treasure of spiritual wisdom that anyone and everyone can count on.

The Founding Father

Francis's emphasis on the possibility of devotion for those living in the world was at odds with the prevailing thought of his day. At that time many people believed that holiness was only possible for those who would withdraw themselves from the world. This religious dualism—splitting the world of God from the human world—was evident in the various forms of religious life in which men and women left the cities for convents and monasteries, there to become holy as only they could do. Here again Francis's novel vision of the world would bring new light.

In 1610, together with Jane de Chantal, Francis founded the Visitation of Holy Mary, a religious order of women whose aim was the life of charity exemplified in the Virgin Mary's visit to her cousin Elizabeth. This new order was uniquely conceived. It was established not on the traditional vows of chastity, poverty, and obedience but always and everywhere on charity: "We have no bond but the bond of love," Francis wrote in the *Book of Profession* (*OEA*, vol. 25, pp. 135–136). Rather than focusing on the stringent practices of mortification common to religious orders of the time, these sisters would actually go out into the city to visit and care for the sick. This new religious lifestyle attracted many women who would not otherwise have been able to join a convent. Older women, widows, disabled women were given access to this way of life. Though for other reasons it eventually became a cloistered order, the Visitation would give rise to apostolic communities of religious and would spread the Salesian spirit in numerous religious orders, secular institutes, and pious societies that still exist today.

This revolution in religious life was inspired by Francis's constant attention to the mystery of God in the ordinary events of human activity. This vision inspired his instructions to the sisters in *The Spiritual Conferences*, as well as the formulation of the *Spiritual Directory* that was at the heart of life in the Visitation communities. In this guide, Francis encourages us to consider the presence of God in every activity of our day, from rising in the morning to sleeping at night. From this *attention* to God, we can then direct our *intention* to serving God well in all that we do. Considering the declining number of religious vocations today, this simple vision enlightens the ever increasing role that laypersons are called to play in the modern world and offers them a practical guide to fulfilling the Christian vocation.

The Saintly Patron

Francis's renown as a spiritual leader, along with the spread of Visitation monasteries to other cities, led him on many travels. His last, in November 1622, was to Avignon where he met with both the king of France and the duke of Savoy. From there the parties journeyed to Lyons where the princes and their courts were welcomed with triumphal fanfare. For his part Francis retired to the hospitality of the Visitation monastery. There, on 28 December, he passed to eternity after fifty-five years on earth, including twenty as the bishop of Geneva.

Francis was beatified only forty years after his death and was canonized by Pope Alexander VII in 1665. His legacy of pastoral solicitude was given appreciation in 1854 when Pope Pius IX declared him Patron of the Deaf. His treasure of spiritual counsel was given approbation in 1877 when the same pope declared him a Doctor of the Church. Finally, his artful ability to communicate the truths of the faith was given recognition in 1923 when Pope Pius XI declared him Patron of Catholic Journalists and of the Catholic Press.

Praying with Francis de Sales

Though his writings are steeped in an inspired understanding of the rudiments of human psychology and the profundity of mystical theology, Francis offers a method of prayer that revolves around three simple aspects. First, he emphasizes the role of the imagination in its ability to produce a consideration of the presence of God. Then, building upon this imagination, he encourages a stirring of affections in the heart that will move the soul to appreciate God's love. Finally, based on this appreciation, he admonishes the one who prays to make practical resolutions as an effective way of bringing this union with God into the various domains of daily living. To give a foundation to the meditations that follow, let us examine each of these pillars of prayer.

The Power of the Imagination

One incontestable fact about Francis's spiritual legacy is his emphasis on beauty as the starting point for all theological reflection. In fact, his writings contain so many images—thirty-three thousand by one scholar's count!—that he is arguably the literary champion of the imagination among all French authors of his time (cf. Lemaire, *Etude des images littéraires de François de Sales,* pp. 15–22). In his poetic writing style, Francis incorporates a whole host of personifications, one-word images, symbols, and stories. We know, too, that his many sermons are filled with illustrations and comparisons drawn from sacred Scriptures, natural history, and the whole range of human activity. In Francis's own words, this use of the imagination affords much benefit because it demonstrates "an inestimable efficacy to enlighten the understanding and move the will" (*On the Preacher and Preaching,* p. 50).

With regard to praying, Francis evidently employed this spiritual imagination in his own life. His *Mystical Exposition on the Canticle of Canticles,* in fact, is an extended flight of his spiritual fancy. He also wholeheartedly counseled others to make use of this properly human faculty as a means of enabling the lively and attentive realization of God's presence. This is necessary, he says, as a means of drawing ourselves into an affective participation in the kind of life presented by the power of the image.

Thus, praying with Francis is a somewhat playful exercise! This does not, however, mean that the imagination in prayer is only a figment of the mind. Rather, Francis's vision of prayer is holistic, encompassing all of the productive powers of the human spirit. This life of prayer, then, is so much more than psychological enthusiasm or theological understanding. In Francis's view, it is a life that flows from and leads back to the very heart of each person.

For Francis, the use of the imagination is fundamental to exciting in the one who prays a passion for the possibility of a new world. By disclosing to our mind and heart the realities of God's redemptive presence, we will be able to approach prayer not as a duty to be fulfilled but as a means of transforming our life in union with the God to whom we pray.

The Centrality of the Heart

This imaginative transformation in prayer is centered in the human heart. There one finds not simply a physical organ but the very principle of human life. In the human heart one recognizes a built-in longing for beauty and goodness, a natural impulse or inclination that stirs the desire of every human person to be directed back to the God of all beauty and goodness. Thus, it is in the divinely inspired beating of the heart that the journey of prayer begins.

In his teaching on prayer, Francis presents union with the heart of God in Jesus as that to which we aspire. It is this divinely personal heart that gives us our spiritual identity, as Wendy M. Wright explains:

> What is the quality of this Christ-heart as Jane and Francis perceived it? The Salesian Jesus is perhaps best seen in a passage in Matthew's gospel which presents the Lord as inviting all to come and learn from him for he is gentle and humble of heart (10:25). From a Salesian perspective this is not a sentimental depiction but one full of vigor and challenge. For the words of this Jesus are part of a discourse in which the mysterious identity of the child of God is revealed as being one of gentleness and humility, an identity that ushers in the reign of God while overturning the values of the world. It is an identity that Salesian spirituality asserts is crucial to the enfleshing of divine life in creation. (Annice Callahan, ed., *Spiritualities of the Heart*, pp. 147–148)

And in Francis's teaching, the means for enfleshing this heart in our life is the twofold movement of love that prayer excites, namely complacence and benevolence. As he explains in *Treatise on the Love of God*:

> Love of complacence draws God into our hearts, but love of benevolence projects our hearts into God and consequently all our actions and affections, which it most lovingly dedicates and consecrates to him. (Vol. 2, p. 60)

In other words, through complacence we are able to apprehend the good of God in other people and in the world around us and take delight in it; through benevolence we choose and will to make that goodness of God grow even more.

The heart, then, is the sacred space in which one prays and by which one lives. As Francis tells Philothea in *Introduction to the Devout Life*:

> I have wished above all else to engrave and inscribe on your heart this holy and sacred motto, "Live, Jesus!" I am certain that your life, which comes from the heart . . . will thereafter produce all its actions—which are its fruits—inscribed and engraved with this sacred word of salvation. As our beloved Jesus lives in your heart, so too he will live in all your conduct and he will be revealed by your eyes, mouth, hands, yes even the hair on your head. (P. 184)

Thus, the art of heartfelt prayer with Francis reaches far beyond the repetition of words and the recitation of formulas. And it bears fruit in a true devotion that can be readily tasted in the practice of virtue.

The "Little Virtues"

For Francis, praying does not end with the last thoughts and words of our conversation with God. Rather, the imaginative transformation of the heart is to be realized fully in the concrete actions of our daily living in the world. This, for Francis, is true devotion: when the human person, moved by prayer, not only does what is good, but does it carefully and promptly, actively and diligently. In Francis's understanding, then, to be devout is both to perform an activity and to cultivate an attitude. It involves the continual practice of charitable deeds, but with the spiritual orientation to do these in loving response to the grace of God within the human soul.

The exercise of this spiritual devotion centers on the fulfillment of God's will made known to us in prayer. For our journey Francis offers us two ways to achieve this lofty goal.

On the one hand, prayer enables us to love God wherever we are. Considering the universal presence of God in this world reborn, wherever we go, there we are, and there God is, too. The circumstances and situations, tasks and duties, people and places that we encounter every day are the spaces in which our life unfolds. By prayer and devotion we can make them sacred places.

On the other hand, prayer also helps us to love God however we can. Considering the life of beauty and goodness to which we are naturally inclined, and the grace of God's own beauty and goodness so generously shared with us, all that we do—whether successful or not—can become holy, provided that we prayerfully intend to do each and every one of these acts for the love of God.

For Francis, this twofold attitude, cultivated through our prayer, yields an approach to life that welcomes every opportunity to show our love for God. As he says in *Introduction to the Devout Life:*

> Occasions do not often present themselves for the exercise of fortitude, magnanimity, and great generosity, but meekness, temperance, integrity, and humility are virtues that must mark all our actions in life. We like sugar better than salt but salt is in more common and frequent use. We must always have on hand a good supply of these general virtues since we must use them almost constantly. (Pp. 121–122)

These general virtues may be "little" in terms of public perception but, for the devout soul, they are great in terms of spiritual civility. By putting them into practice, the one who prays with Francis gives human expression to the will of God by being genuinely good to others. And with this prayerful virtue, the world waiting to be born will come to know the love of God that gives it, and us, life.

Heart to Heart

Theme: In the human heart is to be found the principle of human life as it is directed toward God. "Since the heart is the source of our actions, as the heart is so are they" (*Introduction to the Devout Life*, p. 184).

Opening prayer: Dear God, live in our heart, for that is what it is made for; open our heart to receive your love, for that is what we are made for.

About Francis

Amid the legacy of his entire life and thought, the crowning achievement of Francis remains to this day the religious order he founded—the Visitation of Holy Mary.

Traveling to Dijon in 1604 to preach a Lenten series, Francis encountered Jane de Chantal, who had recently become a widow. Strangely enough he recognized her immediately, for in a spiritual vision "Francis had seen Jane as becoming the foundress of a religious congregation that he would have to create one day" (Ravier, *Sage and Saint*, p. 137). That day came on 6 June 1610.

As previously mentioned, Francis envisioned for this new order a unique approach to the religious life. First, the Visitation would welcome any woman who was drawn to follow the natural inclination of her heart toward union with God in prayer, and especially those who, for physical or emotional reasons, would not be accepted in other congregations. Second, the members of this religious institute, unlike other monasteries of the time, would not be strictly cloistered. As a result of the interior union of their own heart with God and as a way of demonstrating the supreme virtue of charity, these sisters would go out into the town to serve the poor and sick. As Francis himself explained:

> Since this congregation does not have as many austerities or as indissoluble bonds as formal orders and regular congregations, the fervor of charity and the force of a deep personal resolution must supply for all that and take the place of laws, vows, and jurisdiction; so that in this congregation might be realized the saying of the Apostle which affirms that charity is the perfect bond. (*OEA,* vol. 25, p. 216; as cited in *Letters of Spiritual Direction,* p. 47)

Pause: Inquire into the religious state of your own heart; is it agitated and troubled or contented and at peace?

Francis's Words

Francis emphasizes that each and every one of us is capable of living the fully spiritual life:

> It is thus by a deep and secret instinct that our heart tends in all its actions towards happiness and reaches out for happiness. It seeks it now here, now there, groping as it were without knowing where it abides or in what it consists until faith reveals it and describes its infinite marvels. Then, when it has found the treasure sought for, ah! what contentment comes to this poor human heart! What joy, what loving complacence! (*Treatise on the Love of God,* vol. 1, p. 142)

Based on this inclination toward the happiness that only God can give, Francis finds the locus of the spiritual life deep within us. In his thought, progress along the spiritual journey is to be made by remaining ever attentive to our interior intimacy with God:

> Once you have resolved to follow your affection . . .
> don't waste time during prayer trying to understand exactly what you are doing or how you are praying; for the
> best prayer is that which keeps us so occupied with God
> that we don't think about ourselves or about what we
> are doing. In short, we must go to prayer simply, in good
> faith, and artlessly, wanting to be close to God so as to
> love Him, to unite ourselves to Him. True love has scarcely any method. (*Letters of Spiritual Direction*, p. 167)

Reflection

While there may be no surefire method to loving someone, we can say that real human love entails the union of hearts and souls. The same is true of prayer, which is nothing else than our loving communication with God breathed forth from the interior of our being and lived out in our relationships with others. Thus, in the Salesian tradition, the spiritual journey does not adhere to some mechanical method but instead follows the impulses of the heart. There God speaks to us by natural inclination, and we learn to respond in kind.

To facilitate this prayerful conversation, Francis recommends that we first place ourselves in the presence of God. This consideration in turn leads to the stirring of our affections by way of the imagination. Then, following from the passion for God excited in us, we resolve to act in a way that brings this love to life. Finally, we should renew our meditation throughout the day by pious thoughts and an examination of our conscience. In this way true devotion will be a continual process whereby "heart speaks to heart" (*OEA*, vol. 12, p. 321) in the affective love of God and the effective love of our neighbor.

✧ In a quiet place, take a moment to breathe . . . slowly and consciously. Listen as the air both fills your lungs (inspiration) and exits your nostrils (respiration). Focus on this life-sustaining process. Feel the God of warmth and light within you. Allow this to clear your head and energize your body. Consider that breathing is not done by your own choice or decision; rather, it is a "spirit" breathing within you—the presence of God.

✧ Picture the heart that is beating within you. Feel its rhythms. Stir your soul to wonder at how this small organ pumps the blood of life throughout your body. Raise your heart to God, who keeps all things in the universe alive.

✧ Imagine the sacred heart of Jesus (or look at a portrayal of it). See how his heart beats like yours yet is so much more. Consider this heart pierced by the soldier's lance. See how its drops of blood are literally poured forth on the earth. Why is it that God loves us so much, even when we humans break that sacred heart? When in your life has your heart been broken? Journal about your thoughts and feelings of Jesus in his passion and death. Journal about your own experiences of brokenheartedness and enduring love and unite them with Jesus' experiences.

✧ Prayerfully read Deuteronomy 10:12–15 and consider the state of your own heart:
+ Imagine that Moses is speaking to you when he asks, "What does the LORD your God require of you?"
+ In what way do you "fear the LORD your God"? Stir your heart to wonder at the awesome mystery of God speaking to you.
+ How do you "walk in all [God's] ways"? Imagine God walking along with you. Ask where you are both going and how you will get there.
+ How do you "keep the commandments of the LORD your God?" If you find these burdensome, ask for God's grace to aid you "for your own well-being."

✧ Resolve to keep God in your heart this day. To demonstrate that affection, create your own greeting card to God. What picture will you put on the cover? What words will you use to express your love?

✧ Repeat often the thought of Saint Augustine: "My heart will not rest until it rests in you, O God." Make this your thought for the day. And when you rest at night, listen once again to that beating heart and breathing spirit. Give thanks to God for having kept you alive this day.

God's Word

Set me as a seal upon your heart,
    as a seal upon your arm;
for love is strong as death,
    passion fierce as the grave.
Its flashes are flashes of fire,
    a raging flame.
Many waters cannot quench love,
    neither can floods drown it.
If one offered for love
    all the wealth of his house,
    it would be utterly scorned.

(Song of Solomon 8:6–7)

Closing prayer:

"O my soul, be ever without rest or tranquillity whatsoever here on this earth, be ever such until at length you have come to the fresh waters of undying life and to God most holy, for they alone can quench your thirst and quiet your desire." (*Treatise on the Love of God,* vol. 1, p. 189)

✧ Meditation 2 ✧

Seeing God in All Things

Theme: "It is not by the multiplicity of things we do that we acquire perfection, but by the perfection and purity of intention with which we do them" (*Spiritual Conferences*, p. 238).

Opening prayer: Oh God, may your divine love impart its sacred movements to all our actions so that we may perform them out of love for you (adapted from *Treatise on the Love of God*, vol. 2, p. 271).

About Francis

During the course of his hectic apostolic life, Francis was known for his ability to remain in constant contact with God, who dwelt in his heart. At the process for his beatification, one witness testified that

> in order to unite himself always to God and to not have his heart and his thoughts carried away by others, this blessed Prelate placed himself very often in the presence of God by acts of recollection, from time to time raising his eyes to heaven. (*Saint François de Sales par les Témoins de sa Vie*, p. 177)

Others who knew him also witnessed Francis's keen ability to focus on God, even amid ordinary activities:

"When I had the pleasure of entering his room, I always found him intent upon God and heavenly things from which nothing seemed capable of drawing him away. I have often eaten at his table, . . . I have often conversed with him and I protest that I never heard him utter anything that did not in some way refer to God or with an unequalled sweetness tend to incite his hearers to the practice of divine love." (*The Spirit of St. Francis de Sales*, p. 27)

For Francis, this continual vision of God's presence in all things generated the practice of directing his intention to fulfilling the will of God in whatever he was doing. Keeping this motive in mind and in heart was the key to his devout life.

Pause: Look around you now. Where is it that you can see the goodness and presence of God?

Francis's Words

Along the spiritual journey with Francis, the practice of recollection is the beginning of prayer:

In prayer we approach God and place ourselves in His presence for two reasons. The first is to render to God the honor and praise we owe Him, and this can be done without His speaking to us or our speaking to Him. . . . The second reason why we present ourselves before God is to speak to Him and to hear Him speak to us through inspirations and the inner stirrings of our heart. (*Letters of Spiritual Direction*, pp. 100–101)

In order to bring this prayer to fulfillment in the actions of our daily life, our recollection should elicit a purposeful intentionality.

They who wish to thrive and advance in the way of our Lord should, at the beginning of their actions, both exterior and interior, ask for his grace and offer to his divine Goodness all the good they will do. In this way they will be prepared to bear with peace and serenity all the pain and suffering they will encounter as coming from the fatherly hand of our good God and Savior. His most holy intention is to have them merit by such means in order to reward them afterwards out of the abundance of his love.

They should not neglect this practice in matters which are small and seemingly insignificant, nor even if they are engaged in those things which are agreeable, and in complete conformity with their own will and needs, such as drinking, eating, resting, recreating and similar actions. By following the advice of the Apostle, everything they do will be done in God's name to please him alone. (*Spiritual Directory of St. Francis de Sales*, pp. 23–24)

By this means Francis assures us of reaching our destination of loving union with God.

Great deeds may not always come our way, but at all times we can do little deeds with perfection, that is, with great love. (Vol. 2, p. 268)

When our intentions are in the love of God as we plan some work or undertake some project, all acts that follow from it take their value and derive their dignity from the dilection that gives them their origin. (*Treatise on the Love of God*, vol. 2, p. 273)

Reflection

Our human nature is unique in that we alone have the ability to interiorize our life: we remember, we ponder, we reflect, we decide. As such, progress on the spiritual journey is first and foremost a matter of intentionality. How and why we do things is important.

Because the spiritual journey is a matter of traveling away from self-love and toward divine love, Francis counsels us to practice the "direction of intention." This brief, prayerful consideration focuses our attention on the presence of God in all things and channels our intentions with great psychological effectiveness. It reminds us that what we do is of only relative importance, because God alone is ultimate. It projects our desire for spiritual growth away from our own self-sufficiency and brings our action into the realm of God's grace. And, in the end, it transforms our desire for self-gratification into a willing acceptance of God's own good pleasure. In this way, we are able to make holy all that we say and do.

✧ Pause for a moment and raise your eyes to heaven. If you can, lay back in an open field or take a walk on a starry night. Consider the vastness of space beyond. Ask yourself, Where is God?

+ Is God in the thunderbolt on a stormy night?
+ Is God in a flood or fire or tornado?
+ Is God within you—in the feeling of comfort when you are afraid, in the affirmation you need when starting a new project, in the reassurance of being human when you make a mistake?

✧ Prayerfully read Psalm 8 and imagine the world as the psalmist does.

+ Look up to the heavens, moon, and stars. Consider your own smallness in this grand cosmos.
+ Look around you to the animals on land, in the air, and below the seas. Consider that among all these living things, you alone stand out as a child of God.
+ How wonderful it is that God loves the unique creature that you are! Lift your voice and give your own praise to God, as Creator of heaven and earth.

✧ Make a calendar of your daily activities. Where, amid your many tasks, can you find time for recollection? Try to schedule breaks in the morning, afternoon, and evening in which you can spend a few quiet moments with God.

✧ Try this simple practice: whenever you sit down to a meal, first offer a toast to God. Say it aloud or think it in silence. In this way you can give attention to God in ordinary events every day.

✧ Read again Francis's instruction from the *Spiritual Directory* in the previous "Francis's Words" section. Compose your own personal "direction of intention." Write this on a small card and carry it with you throughout the day. At the beginning of each task that you undertake, repeat the prayer.

God's Word

I have been crucified with Christ; and it is no longer I who live, but it is Christ who lives in me. And the life I now live in the flesh I live by faith in the Son of God, who loved me and gave himself for me. (Galatians 2:19–20)

So, whether you eat or drink, or whatever you do, do everything for the glory of God. (1 Corinthians 10:31)

Closing prayer:

Heavenly Father, we raise our hearts and minds to you. We see how from eternity your goodness has destined for our salvation all means to progress in your love. May we embrace the good that we will do and the ills that we must suffer, because your providence has eternally willed it so. (Adapted from *Treatise on the Love of God*, vol. 2, p. 274)

✧ Meditation 3 ✧

Thy Will Be Done

Theme: "Provided that the name of God is sanctified, that His majesty reigns in you, and that His will is done, then the soul cares for nothing else" (*Thy Will Be Done,* p. 234).

Opening prayer: Dear God, may we desire nothing here below but you alone and your good pleasure. May we desire all that you desire and only as you desire it. May we be willing to accept all that you may send and to do whatever you may ask.

About Francis

Stories associated with Francis's priestly vocation demonstrate that even from a young age he was particularly attuned to following the will of God.

> After his trip to Chambéry, Francis was returning to La Thuille by way of the Sionnaz Woods, accompanied by Father Déage. Suddenly his horse stumbled and fell. His cavalier's sword came out of its scabbard; the scabbard became detached from the belt in such a way that the sword and the scabbard formed a cross. Francis climbed onto his saddle again. Shortly afterward, there was another fall and a new cross on the ground. And a third time. (Ravier, *Sage and Saint,* p. 50)

Later confirmed by Michel Favre at the process of his beatification, "it is certain that this incident moved Francis to the
extent that, on the spot, he spoke confidentially to Father
Déage about his vocation" (Ravier, *Sage and Saint,* pp. 50–51).

Throughout his life, Francis gave great attention to the
will of God as it was made known in the ordinary events of
daily life.

> "Which would you prefer," he was asked one day, "to live
> in perfect health or to spend the rest of your life a paralyt-
> ic on your bed?" "I would like neither the one nor the
> other," he replied; "I am indifferent, and in one thing or
> the other I wish only the good pleasure of God." "But in
> health you could accomplish more good than if you were
> sick." "I do not wish," he replied, "to choose the manner
> of serving my God; in health I shall serve Him by acting;
> in sickness I shall serve by suffering. It is for Him to
> choose what pleases Him best; either way I shall do His
> will and that is enough for me." (*The Spirit of St. Francis de
> Sales,* p. 59)

Pause: Consider the vocation you have followed and reflect on how it corresponds to the will of God for you.

Francis's Words

For Francis, the perfection of the spiritual life boils down to
only one thing: conforming our will entirely to the will of our
all-good God.

> There are some matters in which it is clear what God's
> will is, as in what concerns the commandments or the du-
> ties of one's vocation. That is why we must always seek to
> carry out well what God expects of all Christians, as well
> as what our own vocation requires of us in particular.
> . . . There are still other matters about which there is no
> doubt whether God wills them, such as trials, illnesses
> and chronic conditions. That is why we should accept
> them with a good heart, and conform our will to that of
> God who permits them. . . . But we must go further and

see this will not only in great afflictions but even in little reversals and minor inconveniences that we will always meet with in this unhappy life. (*Letters of Spiritual Direction*, p. 105)

When one has learned to look at life through the lens of God's will, everything that happens becomes an opportunity for holiness.

Live for God alone. . . . And do not think that Our Lord is any further away from you while you are caught up in the worries attendant on your state of life than he would be if you were enjoying the delights of a tranquil life. No, . . . what brings him near to our hearts is not the tranquillity but the faithfulness of our love, not the feeling we have of his sweetness, but our free consent to his holy will; and it is more desirable that his will should be wrought in us than that we should follow our own inclinations in him. (*Selected Letters*, p. 191)

Here is the most important point: find out what God wants, and when you know, try to carry it out cheerfully or at least courageously; not only that, but we must love this will of God and the obligations it entails, even if it means herding swine the rest of our lives and performing the most menial tasks in the world, because whatever sauce God chooses for us, it should be all the same to us. Therein lies the very bull's eye of perfection, at which we must all aim, and whoever comes nearest to it wins the prize. (*Letters of Spiritual Direction*, p. 109)

Reflection

Because people in love are primarily interested in pleasing the one who is loved, we are best able to love God by fulfilling the divine will. The question, though, is how do we know what God's will is for us?

Francis believed that the will of God is made known to us in two basic ways (cf. *Treatise on the Love of God*, books 8–9). First, there is the "signified will of God." This is God's way of revealing to us how our life *should be:* the Gospels' teachings, the Ten Commandments, the Beatitudes, the evangelical counsels, the teachings of the church. By these means we can be relatively certain of what God wants us to do. The spiritual life, then, is a matter of conforming our will to God's as it is made known to us in these ways.

Second, there is the "will of God's good pleasure." This is God's hand at work in the way life *is.* The situations in which we find ourselves, the successes and failures of our deeds, the joys and pains we experience—in all these conditions we are subject to the totality of God's will. In this realm, the spiritual life is a matter of submitting our wants and desires to the providence of God, who has created and redeemed all the world.

✧ Look back on the extraordinary events of your own life. Can you see the hand of God at work in them? What signs reveal to you the presence of God in these or other situations?

✧ Locate a favorite icon—a picture, wall hanging, statue, or other artwork. Quietly contemplate its features. Make it come alive in your imagination.
+ What thoughts lead you from the image to God?
+ What emotions are stirred within you for God?
+ What does the icon say to you about God?

✧ On a piece of paper, make two columns. On the left side, write out the Ten Commandments (Exodus 20:2–17). On the right side, list those things that may lead you astray from each commandment. Each day choose one of the commandments to follow and plan the best way for you to keep it.

✧ Repeat the same activity for the Beatitudes (Matthew 5:3–11). List the ways in which you can fulfill each one, and practice one each day.

✧ At the end of the day, choose the best and the worst thing that happened to you. Consider how God's will was revealed to you in each of them. Ask yourself how you responded to God's will in each case and plan to respond better the following day.

God's Word

[Jesus] came out and went, as was his custom, to the Mount of Olives; and the disciples followed him. When he reached the place, he said to them, "Pray that you may not come into the time of trial." Then he withdrew from them about a stone's throw, knelt down, and prayed, "Father, if you are willing, remove this cup from me; yet, not my will but yours be done." Then an angel from heaven appeared to him and gave him strength. (Luke 22:39–43)

Closing prayer:

"Oh God, . . . may Thy holy will be done, not only in the execution of Thy commandments, counsels and inspirations which we must obey, but also in suffering the afflictions which come upon us; may Thy holy will do by us, for us, in us and with us whatever is most pleasing and acceptable to it." (*The Spirit of St. Francis de Sales*, pp. 65–66)

The Time Is Now

Theme: "Let us serve God well today. God will provide for tomorrow. Each day must shoulder its own care" (*OEA*, vol. 19, p. 15).

Opening prayer: "'When will it be, O my God, that my soul will follow the attractions of your goodness?'" (*Introduction to the Devout Life*, p. 102).

About Francis

As Bishop of Geneva, Francis's daily life was filled with an assortment of activities that made the present moment of each day his spiritual time for discovering the will of God.

First and foremost, this divine will was to be found in prayer. Each day Francis devoted a whole hour to prayer, sometimes more, and the summit of his devotion was the daily celebration of the Mass. He supplemented this formal prayer with two hours of time reserved to himself for spiritual reading.

But much more of his time was spent on the daily routines associated with the pastoral life. First were the constant business affairs, which "were, to be sure, numerous, complex, and delicate" (Ravier, *Sage and Saint*, p. 120). Then there was the seemingly endless stream of spiritual correspondence. To this was added counseling, teaching catechism classes, hearing confessions, and, of course, preaching.

Yet, despite the potential for distraction that these worthwhile activities posed, Francis found in these very moments the time for God.

> St. Chantal asked him one day if he was for any length of time without thinking of God. "Yes," he replied, "sometimes for the space of a quarter of an hour." (*The Spirit of St. Francis de Sales*, p. 27)

Pause: Consider your own daily calendar. How much of your time is spent in the awareness of the presence of God?

Francis's Words

For Francis, the devout life held neither time nor place for spiritual ambition.

> It seems to me that you have discovered the true source of your problem when you tell me that you have a multitude of desires which you will never be able to accomplish. . . . In vain will you make plans to execute things, the matter of which is not in your power or is indeed at a distance, if you do not execute those at your command. (*OEA*, vol. 12, pp. 181–182)

More often than not, Francis found that the desire for future perfection is something of our own making.

> There are souls who make great plans to perform wonderful services for our Lord by way of lofty deeds and extraordinary sufferings, but they are deeds and sufferings for which no occasion presents itself and perhaps will never present itself. In making such plans they think that they have performed a great feat of love, but in that they are very often deceived. This is shown by the fact that while they embrace by desire, as they think, great future crosses, they carefully shirk the burden of lesser crosses actually present. (*Treatise on the Love of God*, vol. 2, p. 268)

For Francis, living in the present moment is the way to carry out our journey to God.

> Our Lord does not want you to think either about your progress or about your improvement in any way whatever; but to receive and use faithfully the occasions of serving him and of practising the virtues at every moment, without any reflection either on the past or on the future. Each present moment should bring its task, and the only thing we have to do as we turn towards God is to abandon ourselves utterly to him and long for him to destroy everything in us that opposes his plans. (*Selected Letters,* p. 158)

Reflection

"There is no time like the present"—this is not only an effective truth for time management but also a pillar of stability for the spiritual life. By focusing on the present moment, we are able to avoid two extremes: living in the past, where we are often weighed down by previous failures or missed opportunities; and yearning for the future, where we can easily drift away to daydreaming about what is not yet (or not ever) real. This spiritual journey may be a long road to follow, but where we have come from and where we are going is not nearly as important as where we are, for God is surely to be found there.

✧ Read prayerfully the Gospel story of those who wished to follow Jesus (Luke 9:57–62) and imagine that you are standing there among the listeners. Consider the Lord's comments as they apply to your own life:
+ How far would you be willing to follow Jesus?
+ Are there other tasks that keep you from following Jesus?
+ Are there other people who keep you from following Jesus?

✧ Consider the "crosses" you carry. Are they great or small? Are they of your own choosing or of God's choosing? How do you carry your crosses and how could you carry them better?

✧ Ponder the "present moments" when God is with you: when you stop to speak to people instead of rushing off to your other tasks, when you pause to admire a beautiful garden, when you get a smile or a hug from someone. When else is God working for you and within you?

✧ Try this little experiment in the laboratory of the spiritual sciences. Choose one full hour of a day. Go someplace where you are sure not to be distracted. Spend that hour in complete silence—no radio or television, no conversations, no activity.
+ Can you empty your mind of constant thinking?
+ Are you able to really listen to the God within you?
+ What feelings and emotions do you find being stirred up within you?
+ After this time do you find yourself more at peace?

✧ Obtain a watch or clock that you can set to beep or chime on every hour. Each time you hear the sound, say to yourself the following prayer: "I am now one hour closer to eternity. Christ, be merciful to me at that last hour."

God's Word

I am confident of this, that the one who began a good work among you will bring it to completion by the day of Jesus Christ. . . . And this is my prayer, that your love may overflow more and more with knowledge and full insight to help you to determine what is best, so that in the day of Christ you may be pure and blameless, having produced the harvest of righteousness that comes through Jesus Christ for the glory and praise of God. (Philippians 1:6–11)

Closing prayer: My God, may we be what we are and always be that well, to pay honor to you whose craft we are. May we be what you want and not be what we want against your will (adapted from *OEA*, vol. 13, pp. 53–54).

✧ Meditation 5 ✧

Planning for Holiness

Theme: "'Let us all belong to God . . . in the midst of so much busyness brought on by the diversity of worldly things.'" (*OEA*, vol. 14, p. 339; as cited in *Letters of Spiritual Direction*, p. 45)

Opening prayer:

For God alone my soul waits;
for my hope comes from God,
who alone is my rock, my stronghold, my fortress.
I stand firm.
In God is my salvation and glory,
the rock of my strength.

(Psalm 62:5–7)

About Francis

Francis's journey toward holiness took shape at an early age. At only twenty-one years of age, he went to Padua to study law. There, too, he would begin to develop his plan for leading a devout life.

Padua was the second-oldest university town in Europe. Renowned for its Renaissance air, and particularly for its faculties in mathematics, law, and medicine, the university drew over twenty thousand students from all over the continent. Such an influx of youth made the city a place of worldly pleasure, and of the violence that so often accompanies such indulgence. "In short, this environment was hardly propitious to Francis's desire to nurture the spiritual life" (*Spiritual Exercises*, p. 10). Yet, while he was there, Francis initiated a personal plan for holiness.

> With Possevino, Francis worked out a series of "Spiritual Exercises" whereby he could cultivate devotion in the midst of the dissipated world of student life in which he found himself. By means of these exercises, Francis sought to journey safely through this world without losing his way or taking a wrong step. (*Spiritual Exercises*, p. 11)

The first of these exercises, called the "Preparation of the Day," was designed by Francis to help him derive maximum spiritual benefit from the opportunities to do God's will as these were made present to him in the course of a given day. This exercise was later added by Jane de Chantal to the 1628 edition of the *Spiritual Directory*, which to this day inspires the life of the Visitation order.

Pause: Consider your daily routine. What things occur regularly or happen constantly in which you might be able to find God?

Francis's Words

> It is a good thing to aim in a general way at the greatest perfection of Christian life but we should not philosophize about it in detail, unless to consider how we may amend ourselves and advance in the course of the ordinary, everyday happenings of our life; and from one day to the next we should entrust our general wish for perfection to God's providence; and as we look to him for this, we should cast ourselves into God's arms like a little child who in order to grow, simply eats what its father provides day by day, hoping that he will provide according to its appetite and need. (*Selected Letters*, p. 162)

I don't mean that we shouldn't head in the direction of perfection, but that we mustn't try to get there in a day, that is, a mortal day, for such a desire would upset us, and for no purpose. In order to journey steadily, we must apply ourselves to doing well the stretch of road immediately before us on the first day of the journey, and not waste time wanting to do the last lap of the way while we still have to make it through the first. (*Letters of Spiritual Direction*, p. 97)

We forget the maxims of the saints who have given us the advice that each day we must think about beginning our advancement in perfection. . . . It is never finished. We must always begin again, and begin again willingly. . . . What we have done up to the present is good but what we shall begin will be better. When we have finished this, we shall begin another thing which will be still better, and then another, until we depart from this world to begin another life which will have no end, because nothing better could happen to us. (*OEA*, vol. 16, p. 312)

Reflection

Concerned as we are by the great variety of tasks we must accomplish, we risk losing our focus on doing the will of God. The following activity of preparing the day in the presence of God, adapted from Francis's writings, can keep us on track and steer us carefully along the way. Try it at the beginning of your day!

✧ **Invocation.** Invoke the help of God and ask God to make you worthy to spend the day with God without offending God. You may wish to read Psalm 129 or 143.

✧ **Foresight.** Use your imagination to preview or conjecture all that could happen during the course of the day.

✦ Consider the places you will go, the people you will meet, and the things you will do.

✦ With the help of God's grace, wisely and prudently anticipate those occasions that may take you by surprise.

✧ **Disposition.** Carefully plan and then seek out the best means for spending the day doing God's will. Arrange in an orderly fashion those things that would be proper for you to say and do this day.

✦ What will you avoid, and what will you pursue?

✦ In what manner will you accomplish your tasks?

✦ What attitude will you bring to your work?

✦ What will you say in the company of others?

✧ **Resolution.** Make a firm resolution to obey the will of God, especially during the present day. You may wish to read Psalm 62 or 99.

✧ **Recommendation.** Entrust yourself and all of your concerns into the hands of God's eternal goodness and ask God to consider you as always so commended. Leave to God the complete care of who you are and what God wants you to be. You may wish to read Psalm 31 or 40.

God's Word

If Yahweh does not build the house,
in vain do the builders toil;
if Yahweh does not guard the city,
in vain do the sentries watch.
In vain you rise early
and delay going to bed,
toiling to make a living,
since Yahweh provides for the beloved as they sleep.

(Psalm 127:1–2)

Closing prayer:

To you I lift my soul;
show me the way I should go.
I look to you for protection, O God.
Rescue me from my enemies.
You are my God—
teach me to do your will.
May your good spirit
guide me on a safe path.

(Psalm 143:8–10)

✧ Meditation 6 ✧

Recognizing the Gift

Theme: "Bearing with the imperfections of our neighbour is one of the chief characteristics of [holy] love" (*Spiritual Conferences*, p. 66).

Opening prayer: Dear God, make our relationships so firm, cordial, and solid that we will never refuse to do or to suffer anything for the good of our neighbor.

About Francis

The plan for holiness that Francis initiated in Padua carried through to his ministry as a bishop. Another part of that plan was his rule for social gatherings, a simple exercise in which he was able to transform being nice into being devout.

We see this principle in action in the way Francis dealt with the prestigious people of his day. As Jane de Chantal testified:

Our holy bishop was outstanding for his courteous attitude [*civilité*] to others; I know that certain gentlemen of the court particularly admired him for his virtue of accomplished courtesy. There was a holy seriousness, even majesty about all he did, and yet his attitude was at the same time so humble and god-fearing that the hearts of all he conversed with turned towards him with high regard, respect and love. (Elisabeth Stopp, ed., *St. Francis de Sales: A Testimony by St. Chantal*, pp. 140–141)

Even more so, we see this virtue of cordiality in his approach to the common folk who graced the episcopal parlors:

The immense charity of the holy bishop made no distinction between little and great, rich and poor. The ordinary people, peasants, rustics and even the uncouth, were welcomed by him. They spoke to him confidently about their little affairs and he, not causing even a suspicion that his goodness was being imposed upon, listened kindly to everything they had to say, however insipid or tiresome the conversation might be; and his replies were so full of sweetness that they went away happy. . . .

The Bishop of Belley tells how he waited with several persons for a long time to see the holy prelate; he was listening to a poor blind beggar woman, and when they expressed their surprise at the length of the conversation he had held with her, the holy bishop replied: "Ah, this poor blind woman sees the things of God clearer than some others who have good eyes, and I was pleased to entertain her." It was in fact a pleasure for him to converse with simple souls, and his heart, at ease in their company, expanded with delight. (*The Spirit of St. Francis de Sales*, pp. 110–111)

Welcoming others, because they shared the gift of being created in God's image and likeness, was so important to Francis that he specifically instructed his staff to be courteous and deferential to those who came to visit him; they were not to send any of them away, particularly if they were weary from travel or were suffering some other affliction. (*St. François de Sales par les Témoins de sa Vie*, p. 167)

In fact, Francis's cordial attentiveness to all those he met was such that one would think he had nothing else to do!

Pause: Consider those persons whom you meet on a daily basis: Could you be more cordial and welcoming to them?

Francis's Words

In the fourth of his "Spiritual Exercises," Francis highlights the basic principles of religious civility that can be adopted in all affairs.

> I will never disdain meeting any person, no matter who they may be, nor will I show any sign of wishing to avoid them, for this earns one the reputation of being proud, haughty, unfeeling, arrogant, snobbish, ambitious, and manipulative. . . . Above all, I will be careful neither to criticise, nor to mock, nor to be sarcastic to, anyone. It is a sign of stupidity to make fun of those who have no reason to put up with such treatment. I will show great respect for all, and I will not be pretentious. I will speak little but well, so rather than boring my friends I will whet their appetite for further conversation at a later time.
>
> With either friends or acquaintances, I will be especially careful to observe this rule: Be friendly with all but familiar with few. . . . Therefore in my relationships I will be courteous and not overbearing, friendly and outgoing and not cool and reserved, gentle but not affected, compliant and not contradictory (unless reason requires it), sincere and not deceitful, because people want to have a true knowledge of those with whom they are dealing. (*Spiritual Exercises,* pp. 36–37)

Speaking to the sisters of the Visitation, Francis explains the fundamental rationale for this approach to dealing with others, be they social acquaintances or personal friends:

> It is to those who have the most need of us that we ought to show our love more especially, for in such cases we give a better proof that we love through charity than in loving those who give us more consolation, than trouble.
> . . . It is not in our power to have as tender and sweet an affection for those whose tempers and dispositions are not in accordance with our own, as for others with whom we are in sympathy. But that is nothing; it remains that the love of charity must be universal, and the signs and manifestations of our friendship must be

impartial, if we wish to be true servants of God. (*Spiritual Conferences*, pp. 62, 69)

Reflection

As more communication takes place by way of computers and other technologies, avoiding true human interaction becomes easier. Yet, if we recognize that only human beings—and all human beings—have been created in the image and likeness of God, then each time we meet someone we have the opportunity of encountering something of God. And how we treat the persons we do see becomes a good measure of how well we love the God whom we cannot see.

✧ Consider the miracle of childbirth.
✦ Arouse your wonder and amazement at the divinely graced process whereby two cells unite and grow into a living human being.
✦ Contemplate the uniqueness of every child that is born. Give thanks to God for your own uniqueness.
✦ Spend fifteen minutes in a place where you can inconspicuously watch others walk by. In your heart, say to each one, "God has made you who you are."
✦ Let your heart be joyful at the variety and goodness of life.

✧ Read prayerfully the Gospel story of the disciples' concern for greatness in the Reign of God (Mark 9:30–37).
✦ Imagine that you are one of the arguing disciples. How do you picture "greatness"? How would this coincide with Jesus' prediction of betrayal, suffering, and death?
✦ Next, imagine that you are the little child whom Jesus places in their midst and then takes in his arms. How does being embraced by Jesus make you feel? How will you be more welcoming toward others?

✧ Consider your place of work. How could you be more cordial to your colleagues? Do you greet people, on the phone or face-to-face, in a way in which they will remember you for being personable? Do you treat others as images of God? Recall throughout your day Francis de Sales's image of himself in public life: "'[I am] like a fountain in the marketplace'" (*Selected Letters*, p. 21).

✧ Try this social experiment. Spend half a day saying "hello" to every single person you pass without waiting for them to greet you first. Spend the other half a day not saying "hello" to anyone. When the day is over, think about what happened.
+ How did you feel greeting or ignoring others?
+ How did those other people react to you?
+ Ponder how simple greetings might make society a friendlier place.

God's Word

We who are strong ought to put up with the failings of the weak, and not to please ourselves. Each of us must please our neighbor for the good purpose of building up the neighbor. . . . May the God of steadfastness and encouragement grant you to live in harmony with one another, in accordance with Christ Jesus, so that together you may with one voice glorify [God]. Welcome one another, therefore, just as Christ has welcomed you, for the glory of God. (Romans 15:1–7)

Closing prayer: God our creator, help us to be open to your presence in all whom we meet. Give us your grace so that we may neither speak what is ill nor do what is wrong to others, but instead learn to love our neighbors out of love for you.

The Bond of Friendship

Theme: "Love everyone with a deep love based on charity . . . but form friendships only with those who can share virtuous things with you" (*Introduction to the Devout Life*, p. 174).

Opening prayer: Dear God, empty our hearts of all multiplicity so that through our friendships there will dwell in our heart only the sovereign love that unites your Holy Trinity (adapted from *OEA*, vol. 18, p. 235).

About Francis

With many persons Francis demonstrated a familiar and cordial bearing. With some, however, he entered into a holy friendship that would serve as an example of how human love issues from and returns to the love of God.

According to André Ravier, Francis's endearing letters suggest that he "walks step by step, searches, asks, probes, questions, suffers, hopes, prays with Philothea and Theotimus, and he only feels completely at ease when he becomes with his correspondent 'one heart, one soul, and one spirit'" (*François de Sales Correspondance: Lettres d'amitiés spirituelles*, p. x). But beyond this spiritual director's relationship, Francis also enjoyed truly close human friendships. In his youth he was befriended by Antoine Favre, a powerful diplomat, from whom he would receive benevolent support in his missionary endeavors and with whom he would found the Florimontane Academy. Later in life Francis met Vincent de Paul, with whom he enjoyed many profound spiritual discussions. It was to him that Francis would entrust the task of ministering to the sisters of the Visitation in Paris.

But the most profound and exemplary of his holy friendships was shared with Jane de Chantal. In one of his first letters to her after they met, Francis discloses the prayerful foundation of their relationship and intimates the hopeful future of this sacred bond:

> This letter will assure you again and all the more that I shall very carefully keep the promise I made of writing you as often as I can. The greater the physical distance between us, the closer I feel is our interior bond. I shall never stop praying God to perfect His work in you. . . . I beg you never to forget me, since God has given me such a strong determination never to forget you either. (*Letters of Spiritual Direction*, pp. 123, 125)

Not to be forgotten in any of the over four hundred letters he wrote to her was their reciprocal affection, their supportive concern, and, ultimately, their shared crosses in journeying together to God.

> This friendship, born of their common love of God, was nurtured by their shared delight in each other's spiritual gifts and their mutual quest for perfection. Over the next six years the two of them discerned together both the future of Madame de Chantal's spiritual aspirations and the shape of a new project [the Visitation] that would speak to the dreams of both their hearts. (*Letters of Spiritual Direction*, p. 26)

By all accounts, then, Francis's soulful relationship with Jane gives witness to "the birth, development, and flowering of one of the greatest friendships that ever bound a director and his disciple" (Ravier, *Sage and Saint*, p. 137).

Pause: Consider those with whom you are good friends. What makes your relationship so special?

Francis's Words

Francis's own friendships reveal the truth of his teaching that

> all the greatest servants of God have had very particular friendships without doing any harm to their perfection. . . . Hence perfection consists not in having no friendships, but in having only those which are good, holy, and sacred. (*Introduction to the Devout Life*, pp. 176–177)

These perfecting relationships bear the three essential characteristics of any friendship:

> All love is not friendship, first, because we can love without being loved. In such cases there is love but not friendship since friendship is mutual love, and if it is not mutual it is not friendship. Secondly, it is not sufficient for it to be merely mutual. Persons who love each other must be aware of their reciprocal affection and if they are unaware of their love it is not friendship. Thirdly, there must also be some kind of communication between them, and this is the basis of friendship. . . . If they are true goods [that are communicated], the friendship is true, and the better the goods are, the better is the friendship. (*Introduction to the Devout Life*, pp. 169–170)

For Francis, the communication between true friends is marked by an honest and sincere openness. By discussing how God nourishes and sustains their affections, by confiding worries and apprehensions, by demonstrating compassion toward one another, in this and in all the good and holy communication that takes place between friends who are joined together by God, a bond is established that cannot be separated by distance or time (cf. *OEA*, vol. 11, pp. 38–40; vol. 18, p. 416).

Ultimately, the depth to which friends share their spiritual goods leads to an eternal union.

> If your mutual and reciprocal exchanges concern charity, devotion, and Christian perfection, O God, how precious this friendship will be! It will be excellent because it comes from God, excellent because it leads to God, excellent because its bond will endure eternally in God. How

good it is to love here on earth as they love in heaven and to learn to cherish one another in this world as we shall do eternally in the next! (*Introduction to the Devout Life*, pp. 174–175)

Reflection

The complexities of interpersonal relationships are perhaps the most gripping events in our life. Amid the many relationships that characterize our existence, that of true friendship is both rare and precious. To find a best friend—one with whom we can be totally who we are and can share completely who we are—is a great gift from God.

In the bonds of true friendship that we form here on earth, we are able to see and to show that God, who is love, is indeed alive in our midst. And since true devotion is concerned more with relationships than with techniques, the union of hearts begun in human friendship serves as a mirror and a foretaste of the final union we hope for with God.

✧ "'God [has] given me to you,'" wrote Francis de Sales to Jane de Chantal (*Letters of Spiritual Direction*, p. 153). Go for a slow walk or just sit quietly reflecting on the person or persons in your life to whom you could say this. Keep their faces in your imagination. When you have savored this memory sufficiently, reflect on the person or persons who could say these words to you. Imagine them walking or sitting with you now. In the last lap of your walk or in the final moments of your quiet, thank God for these persons in your life.

✧ Recall different friends you have had during your life. Each day for a week post a photograph, reread a letter, or set out a small gift that recalls their providential presence in your life. Remember the good that they brought to you at the time you knew them well. Pray for the blessings they may need today.

✧ Call to mind the relationship you have now with a best friend. Consider the things you share together, those that are joyful and those that are sorrowful. Imagine how God loves you infinitely more than any friend ever could.

✦ If speaking to your friend brings you happiness, how much more will praying to God bring you?

✦ If you and your friend are able to forgive one another, how much greater is God's mercy?

✦ If your friendship has grown with time, how much joy will there be in eternity with God?

✧ Even from friends we keep secrets. Do you have hidden thoughts and feelings, dreams and aspirations that you can disclose to God alone? List these in your spiritual journal and share them with your divine friend.

✧ Prayerfully read the words of Jesus to the disciples in John 15:11–17 and imagine that Jesus is speaking them to you.

✦ What "joy" will make you "complete"?

✦ For whom or for what would you be willing to "lay down [your] life"?

✦ Do you show your friendship with Jesus by doing what he commands you?

✦ What things would you ask God in Jesus' name that God may give you?

✧ In the story of *The Little Prince,* by Antoine de Saint-Exupéry, a young man journeys through the solar system. (If you can, read the story or watch the video.) In his travels the prince eventually learns what it means to be a friend to the flower on his own planet. Consider this wonderful fable in light of your own journey.

✦ What are the real matters of consequence in your relationships, and for what are you responsible?

✦ How has God, the divine prince, "tamed" you?

✦ For the little prince "'it is only with the heart that one can see rightly; what is essential is invisible to the eye'" (p. 70). Make this your thought for the day. Write in your spiritual journal those things you believe to be essential to your friendship with God.

God's Word

Faithful friends are a sturdy shelter:
    whoever finds one has found a treasure.
Faithful friends are beyond price;
    no amount can balance their worth.
Faithful friends are life-saving medicine;
    and those who fear [God] will find them.
Those who fear [God] direct their friendship aright,
    for as they are, so are their neighbors also.

                                      (Sirach 6:14–17)

Closing prayer:

Holy Friend, you have made us such that we love and long for a union of hearts. May the infinite friendship which obtains between you and your Son, through the power of the Spirit, enlighten and guide all our friendships, so that we might always give praise to you, our most unique God. (Adapted from *Treatise on the Love of God*, vol. 1, p. 196)

✧ **Meditation 8** ✧

Nothing Small
in the Service of God

Theme: "It is better to want little than to have much" (*Saint François de Sales par les Témoins de sa Vie*, p. 160).

Opening prayer: Dear God, make us true children of yours, in all innocence and simplicity.

About Francis

In his many dealings with people from all walks and states in life, including his closest friends, Francis was guided by what he called the "little virtues." The first of these is simplicity.

Ever one to seek the truth of God's holy will, Francis was known for his frank and simple approach to social relationships.

> On another occasion the Bishop of Belley expressed his astonishment that the Duke of Savoy did not engage our saint as diplomat at the foreign courts, especially in France, where he enjoyed so great a reputation for prudence, probity and piety. "On the contrary," replied the saint, "I think that the Duke of Savoy in not employing me, gives evidence of wisdom and judgment, for the very

words, human prudence and policy, make me shudder. To speak frankly I do not know how to lie or to dissimulate or to feign adroitly and this is policy's principal resort. I would not for the whole kingdom utter a false word; I speak the ancient Gallic, simple and in good faith; my lips express my thoughts." (*The Spirit of St. Francis de Sales*, p. 179)

This simplicity of expression was most evident in Francis's personal life, where only what was necessary was good enough for him. As Jane de Chantal testifies:

> He told me that if it hadn't worried his servants he would have waited on himself. He loved a humble way of life and practised it at every turn, for instance in his clothes, his furniture and all his belongings. Here in Annecy he was lent a house with large apartments, spacious reception rooms and wide galleries. From the beginning he had his bed tucked away in a very small closet. "And then," as he said to me, "when I've walked about in these grand rooms and galleries all day like a prelate, I can come in here at night and be housed like the poor little man I really am." His valet, François Favre, said in his testimony that the closet was so small that the servants found it difficult to make the bed, a rickety old one inherited from his predecessor. There was no other furniture. On the wall over the bed hung a small silver holy water stoup and a picture of the Child Jesus. (Stopp, ed., *A Testimony by St. Chantal*, p. 86, n. 1)

It was this simplicity, in lifestyle and in deed, which endeared Francis to kings and commoners alike. And this little virtue, so beloved by Francis, would later become one of the distinguishing characteristics of the Visitation order (cf. *Letters of Spiritual Direction*, pp. 67–69).

Pause: Consider your own lifestyle. What things do you really need, and what could you do without?

Francis's Words

As with the other little virtues, Francis defines simplicity in terms of the love of God:

> Simplicity is nothing else than an act of pure and simple charity, having one only aim and end, which is to acquire the love of God, and our soul is simple when in all that we do or desire we have no other aim. (*Spiritual Conferences*, p. 212)

Such a "simple" aim keeps our feet securely on the path of our spiritual journey.

> Sometimes it happens that those who imagine themselves to be angels are not even good men and there is more sublimity in their words and expressions than in their way of thought and deeds. . . . Let us keep to our lower but safer way. It is less excellent but better suited to our lack and littleness. If we conduct ourselves with humility and good faith in this, God will raise us up to heights that are truly great. (*Introduction to the Devout Life*, pp. 127–128)

On the way to this spiritual greatness, simplicity enables the devout soul to accept God's will as it comes.

> The soul which has attained perfect simplicity has only one love, which is for God. . . . It is true that such a soul never neglects any good opportunity which it meets with on its way, but it does not hunt about eagerly for means of perfecting itself other than those which are prescribed. (*Spiritual Conferences*, p. 226)

In so traveling, the simple soul benefits from Francis's simple wisdom!

> Simplicity banishes from the soul that solicitous care, which so needlessly urges many to seek out various exercises and means to enable them, as they say, to love God, and which makes it impossible for them to be at peace if they are not doing all that the saints did. Poor souls! they torment themselves about finding out the art of loving God, not knowing that there is none except to love Him. (*Spiritual Conferences*, p. 214)

Reflection

The spiritual journey presupposes neither tremendous resources nor incredible talent. It demands of us neither heroic tasks nor superstar performances. It is, after all, a simple journey, following the love of God that attracts us and living the will of God that inspires us.

How often do we clutter our earthly trip with the excess baggage of jeweled materials or grandiose plans. How much more effectively could we serve God if only we would simplify our life!

"Love God and do as you will," the great Saint Augustine once said. By refocusing on what is essential, taking delight in being loved by God, and loving other people for the love of God, our spiritual journey to God becomes an easier road to travel.

✧ Prayerfully read the story about Jesus' scourging in Matthew 27:27–31. Imagine what it would feel like to be stripped in public.

◆ How protective are you of exposing your innermost self to others? To God?

◆ How do you react when others mistreat you, when they mock you, jeer at you, or strike out at who you are?

◆ How does the simplicity of Jesus in this scene provide a model for your own action?

✧ Examine your conscience with regard to diplomacy in your relationships. Are you prone to lie in order to protect your own turf? Do you dissimulate or feign the truth as a subtle means for gaining an advantage over others?

✧ Consider the last will and testament you have made with regard to your material possessions. Imagine that you had to divest yourself of those things now and still live. To whom would you give the things you no longer need? To whom would you give the things you still do need? After you have done this pencil-and-paper inventory, think seriously about what you should dispose of now. How are you being called to simplify your lifestyle?

✧ Try a little spring cleaning of your spiritual life. Sort out all the important and not so important things in the house of your soul. What sort of clutter can you discard now? Write these things down on separate pieces of paper and, as a symbol of simplifying your spiritual abode, toss them away.

✧ Create for yourself a personal tabernacle, a box or other container that you can decorate with things that are especially important to you in your relationship with God. Keep only those things that are small and special. Each day as you visit these things, remind yourself of the virtue of simplicity and that there is nothing small in the service of God.

✧ Take as your thought for the day the words of Saint Augustine, "Love God and do as you will." Make an entry in your journal as to how this helps you to simplify your life.

God's Word

Now as they went on their way, [Jesus] entered a certain village, where a woman named Martha welcomed him into her home. She had a sister named Mary, who sat at the Lord's feet and listened to what he was saying. But Martha was distracted by her many tasks; so she came to him and asked, "Lord, do you not care that my sister has left me to do all the work by myself? Tell her then to help me." But the Lord answered her, "Martha, Martha, you are worried and distracted by many things; there is need of only one thing. Mary has chosen the better part, which will not be taken away from her." (Luke 10:38–42)

Closing prayer: Gracious God, in our life's journey, help us to go on our way simply, straightforwardly, openly, and with a child's naivete, sometimes led by your providential hand, other times carried in your loving arms.

✧ Meditation 9 ✧

Patience with All

Theme: "The more perfect our patience the more completely do we possess our [own] souls" (*Introduction to the Devout Life*, p. 128).

Opening prayer: Dear God, give us patience so that while we are here on earth we may go on bearing with ourselves until you bear us up to heaven.

About Francis

Because in Francis's simple approach to the spiritual life, nothing is small in the service of God, his everyday dealings with other people often yielded many occasions to practice virtue. This was especially so with regard to the virtue of patience.

Because of his prominent position, Francis was not immune to persecution from others. He, too, had enemies whose bitterness manifested itself in slander.

> An ecclesiastic who had been refused an unjust claim to a vicarship for which he was not competent, had the insolence to publish a scurrilous lampoon against the honour of the bishop and those closest to him. He actually presented the pamphlet to him when he was seated on his throne in the cathedral church. The Blessed took it, and when he had got back home, he read it calmly and then

took no further notice of it, nor would he allow the priests of his chapter to follow up the matter in any way; they were all for punishing such insolence. Later on he did this same man many good turns, lavishing kindness on him and paying him honour which he little deserved. It was his rule, then, to bear with his neighbor to the utmost, and he taught those whom he directed to do the same. If we were the losers, he said, then God himself would make it up to us generously. . . . "People must be patient with one another," he said, "and the most gallant are those who put up best with other people's shortcomings." (Stopp, ed., *A Testimony by St. Chantal*, p. 91)

Putting up with others, however, first requires the ability to be patient with oneself. For Francis, this was indeed a challenge. Francis was, admittedly, prone to lose his patience. Yet, as Jane de Chantal points out:

I have never heard of anyone who saw him lose his temper. One day I asked him to get just a little worked up about various setbacks we were having in connection with our Visitation monastery here, but all he said was: "Do you really want me to throw away in a quarter of an hour the little bit of control I've painfully managed to acquire over twenty years?" (Stopp, ed., *A Testimony by St. Chantal*, p. 95)

Pause: Consider your daily routines. What opportunities do you have to practice patience?

Francis's Words

For Francis, patience is a virtue that can be practiced in almost every situation of our daily life.

Be patient not only with regard to the big, chief part of the afflictions that may come to you but also as to things accompanying them and accidental circumstances. Many people would be ready to accept evils provided they were not inconvenienced by them.

The truly patient man neither complains of his hard lot nor desires to be pitied by others. He speaks of his sufferings in a natural, true, and sincere way, without murmuring, complaining, or exaggerating them. (*Introduction to the Devout Life*, pp. 129, 130)

This virtue is also suited to the particular quest of our spiritual life.

Have patience with everyone, but chiefly with yourself; I mean to say, do not trouble yourself about your imperfections, and always have the courage to lift yourself out of them. I am well content that you begin again every day: there is no better way to perfect the spiritual life than always to begin again and never to think you have done enough. (*Thy Will Be Done*, p. 49)

By thus developing patience every day, we advance steadily on the spiritual journey toward perfection.

To possess fully our souls is then the effect of patience; and in proportion as patience is perfect, the possession of the soul becomes more entire and excellent. Now, patience is more perfect as it is less mixed with disquiet and eagerness. May God then deign to deliver you from these two troubles, and soon afterward you will be free altogether. (*Thy Will Be Done*, p. 205)

Reflection

One of the paradoxes of the spiritual journey is that cultivating the virtue of patience requires patience! This is why we must practice patience with ourselves first: interiorly, in regulating our natural human temperament, and exteriorly, in learning to accommodate ourselves to the situations and conditions that characterize our existence.

Patience is needed, too, for the spiritual journey itself, for more often than not we will end up taking one step backward for every two steps forward. Nevertheless, as long as we are making progress, speed is not paramount. And once we begin to accept our own place on the journey, we will be in a better position to show patience to others along the way. Like the other virtues, patience is a particular quality that, once developed, can enrich the totality of our life.

✧ Upon coming to the city of Jerusalem, Jesus lamented: "'Jerusalem, Jerusalem, the city that kills the prophets and stones those who are sent to it! How often have I desired to gather your children together as a hen gathers her brood under her wings, and you were not willing!'" (Matthew 23:37).

✦ Consider the crimes against God and our neighbor that have been committed throughout the history of the world. Ask forgiveness of God for the part that you have played in this history.

✦ Imagine God now looking down upon today's cities and seeing the violence that characterizes urban existence. Ask for the grace to be a peacemaker in your hometown.

✦ Consider the patience of God, who desires to gather us together for all eternity. Give thanks to God and resolve to be more patient with God's children all around you.

✧ Make an examination of conscience with regard to your own temper:

✦ What occasions regularly cause you to lose your temper?

✦ Do you find yourself losing your temper more often, or are you more able to hold it in check?

✦ What behaviors usually follow from having lost your temper?

✦ How do others react to your temper?

✧ Create a list of those persons who give you opportunities to practice patience.

✦ What is it about each one that may cause you to lose your patience?

✦ How might you change your ways to show each one more patience?

✦ Offer each of these persons to God and pray for their good.

✧ Which areas of your character need patient attention? Thank God for the "you" that has been created and ask for the grace to grow day by day into the person God wants you to be.

God's Word

Be patient, therefore, beloved, until the coming of the Lord. The farmer waits for the precious crop from the earth, being patient with it until it receives the early and the late rains. You also must be patient. Strengthen your hearts, for the coming of the Lord is near. Beloved, do not grumble against one another, so that you may not be judged. See, the Judge is standing at the doors! As an example of suffering and patience, beloved, take the prophets who spoke in the name of the Lord. Indeed we call blessed those who showed endurance. You have heard of the endurance of Job, and you have seen the purpose of the Lord, how the Lord is compassionate and merciful. (James 5:7–11)

Closing prayer:

Mercifully patient God, with grateful hearts we recall that your Son has saved us by his suffering and endurance. Grant us the patience to work out our salvation by the sufferings and afflictions that occur in our life, and help us to endure with all possible gentleness the injuries, denials, and discomforts we meet. (Adapted from *Introduction to the Devout Life*, p. 128)

✧ Meditation 10 ✧

Lowly but Loved

Theme: Of ourselves we are nothing; all that we have and all that we are come from God (cf. *The Spirit of St. Francis de Sales*, p. 190).

Opening prayer: Dear God, may we have only the pure intention of seeking your honor and glory in all things. Help us to do what little we can toward this, and grant us the grace to leave to you the care of all the rest.

About Francis

Another of the little virtues practiced and commended by Francis, and perhaps the most important, is humility. According to Jane de Chantal, this classic Christian vision attenuated the opinions of Francis's many admirers.

> He was not concerned just to appear humble but he wanted to be truly recognized as a lesser man than people imagined, for he was quite aware that others had a high opinion of him. In this connection he wrote to me one day that after reading a letter of mine, he had paced up and down in his room and tears had started to his eyes at the thought of what he was really like compared with people's imaginary ideas about him, and he used to say that

76

we ought not to think better of ourselves before men than we really were in the sight of God. (*Selected Letters*, p. 157)

Francis's humble vision also counteracted the seemingly natural human propensity to climb ever higher in one's career. Jane de Chantal continues:

It was unheard of for him to take steps to procure any sort of promotion, or important preaching assignments in large towns; on the contrary, he refused several. He had no ambition, as he said, except that he wanted to spend his life working usefully in God's service. . . . I have read a letter in his own hand where he says: "I hear from two quarters that there are plans for making me go up higher in the world; one letter is from Rome, the other from Paris. My answer is now in God's hands: no, you may rest quite assured that I wouldn't lift a little finger for all the world—I take too poor a view of it. If this is not for God's greater glory, the plan will leave me unmoved." (Stopp, ed., *A Testimony by St. Chantal*, p. 87)

This insistent concern for God's glory rather than human honor led Francis to single out humility as the virtue proper to the spiritual life. Jane recalls:

He used to advocate this virtue to everyone in his care, more especially to us of the Visitation. One day when he had entered our enclosure at Lyons to hear the confession of an invalid nun, the sisters put ready a pen, ink and paper on a table in front of him and asked him to write down what he most wanted of us; beginning at the top of the page and writing with great concentration he put down HUMILITY, and that was all. He wanted to show us what he thought of this virtue. (Stopp, ed., *A Testimony by St. Chantal*, p. 86)

Ironically, then, Francis's very determination to live a humble life contributed in no small part to his being honored as a saint!

Pause: Consider your own reputation; compare how you think others see you with how you think God sees you.

Francis's Words

For Francis, the virtue of humility combines recognition of the truth of who we are with the truth of God's love for us.

> Humility is true knowledge and voluntary acknowledgment of our abjection. The chief point of such humility consists not only in willingly admitting our abject state but in loving it and delighting in it. (*Introduction to the Devout Life*, p. 139)

This humility helps us to combat the dangers we typically encounter along the journey toward our own spiritual perfection.

> Why is it that when we happen to commit some imperfection or sin, we are so surprised, upset, and impatient? Without doubt, it is because we thought we were something special, resolute, and steady, and therefore, when we discover that in reality we are nothing of the kind and have fallen flat on our face, we are disappointed, and consequently we are vexed, offended, and upset. If we really knew ourselves well, instead of being astonished at finding ourselves on the ground, we would marvel that we ever manage to remain standing up. That's the other source of our disquiet: we want nothing but consolation and are taken aback when we see and experience our misery, our nothingness, and our weakness. (*Letters of Spiritual Direction*, p. 119)

At the same time, humility makes it possible for us to recognize and accept our companions on this journey.

> Humility makes it possible for us to be untroubled about our own faults by reminding us of those of others; for why should we be more perfect than anyone else? In the same way, why should the shortcomings of others bother us when we recall our own? Why should we find it strange that others have faults when we ourselves have plenty? Humility makes our hearts gentle toward the perfect and the imperfect: toward the perfect, out of respect; toward the imperfect, out of compassion. Humility helps

us to receive afflictions serenely, knowing that we deserve them, and to receive blessings with reverence, knowing that they are undeserved. (*Letters of Spiritual Direction,* p. 121)

Thus, how we see ourselves in relation to how God sees us is for Francis the critical disposition that opens the door for God's entry into the human soul.

Reflection

Religious humility is often misunderstood. But in the Salesian tradition, humility is highly prized as

the recognition of the reality of human dependence upon God, the truth of the profound limitations of the individual person and communities of persons, and the acknowledgment of illusory human pride that strives to be like God and so conspires in its own destruction. . . . Humility is thus not "humiliation" in the negative sense that might be perceived as psychologically unhealthy today. It is rather a recognition of one's own littleness and need in relation to the Creator's immense and lavish abundance. (*Letters of Spiritual Direction,* p. 65)

Humility is also a somewhat paradoxical virtue. The recognition of our lowliness is the admission of the inherent incapability of rising above our mortal limitations on our own. While this admission should rid us of self-destructive pride, it should also fill us with joy in the knowledge that God loves us precisely for who we are and that in the divine goodness we are recipients of God's grace in our journey toward becoming who God wants us to be.

✧ Prayerfully read the account of Jesus' washing the feet of his disciples at the Last Supper (John 13:1–20). Imagine yourself being in the room with the others.

✦ What would your reaction be when Jesus comes to wash your feet? Open your heart and soul to be cleansed by him as well.

✦ What do you think of the Jesus who performs this service? Give thanks to him for making you his beneficiary.
✦ How might you "wash one another's feet"? Resolve to treat others as more important to you than you are to yourself.

✧ Create a diagram that charts the progress you have made in your chosen career.
✦ Where does the chart lead? Where will you be on this "ladder" in five or ten years?
✦ What aspirations do you have in your career? Are these plans "for the glory of God"?
✦ What aspirations do you have in your spiritual life? How do your designs compare with what God wants of you?

✧ Make a list in two columns: on one side, list all those things you consider "afflictions" that you have received; on the other, list those you consider "blessings."
✦ Have you received the afflictions "serenely, knowing that [you] deserve them"?
✦ Have you received the blessings "with reverence, knowing that they are undeserved"?
✦ How might the afflictions be turned into blessings?
✦ Give thanks to God for both lists!

✧ Humility means recognizing the truth about oneself, and yet, we are usually very hard on ourselves. When you receive compliments from friends, do you believe them? Do you appreciate the skills and talents that God has given you? Take some time to write down the things that you like about yourself. Look at what you do for others that makes them happy, even if those things are not glamorous or noteworthy. Before God, give thanks for all that is good about you.

✧ After these examinations, try this exercise. Write two recommendations for the "job" that you are seeking: that of being a devout soul. In the first letter, make yourself the author and give an honest evaluation. In the second letter, make God the author. How do the two letters compare? What can you do to bring the two letters into closer correspondence? Bring your final reflections before a God in whose presence you are both lowly and loved.

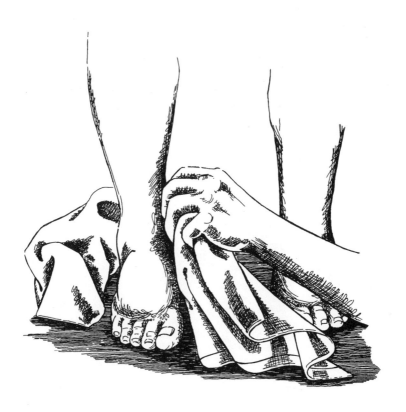

God's Word

Jesus, knowing that [God] had given all things into his hands, and that he had come from God and was going to God, got up from the table, took off his outer robe, and tied a towel around himself. Then he poured water into a basin and began to wash the disciples' feet and to wipe them with the towel that was tied around him. . . .

After he had washed their feet, had put on his robe, and had returned to the table, he said to them, "Do you know what I have done to you? You call me Teacher and Lord—and you are right, for that is what I am. So if I, your Lord and Teacher, have washed your feet, you also ought to wash one another's feet. For I have set you an example, that you also should do as I have done to you. (John 13:3–5,12–15)

Closing prayer: Forgiving God, help us to be lowly, to despise ourselves to the death of all our passions, as your Son did to death on the cross. May we learn to love our misery as a means by which your goodness shows us your mercy (cf. *Selected Letters,* p. 268, and *Thy Will Be Done,* p. 135).

All by Love,
Nothing by Force

Theme: "'The one who can preserve gentleness in the midst of sorrows and sufferings and peace in the midst of the multiplicity and busyness of affairs—that person is almost perfect'" (*OEA,* vol. 17, p. 260; as cited in *Letters of Spiritual Direction,* p. 64).

Opening prayer: Dear God, help us to tame our hearts and train them in gentleness. May we not contest or dispute what comes our way but simply turn our heart back to Jesus Christ crucified and learn to love as he did.

About Francis

The esteem with which people regarded Francis made it easy for them to approach him. And while he welcomed one and all, it was to those most in need of his commiseration that Francis poured out his gentle kindness, even if it was not the politically correct thing to do.

> At times some of his friends were shocked at this manner of acting [welcoming great sinners] and they ventured to reproach him. . . . "But then," someone said, "these are apostates and wicked men, altogether unworthy of your

caresses." On hearing these words his heart was filled with sorrow, and raising his eyes to heaven he cried out: "Alas, there is no one but God and myself to love these poor sinners. I am expected to treat them harshly because they are sinners, as if they were not on that very account more deserving of compassion and tenderness." (*The Spirit of St. Francis de Sales*, pp. 132–133)

This loving gentleness, which flowed directly from his humility, was most evident in Francis's approach in the confessional. There he took to heart the realization that the penitent addresses the confessor as "father," and Francis's paternal care knew no bounds.

He spoke to another penitent who had been leading a very vicious life. "I regard you now as a saint," said he. "But," she replied, "your conscience tells you the opposite." "No, not at all," said he, "I am speaking according to my conscience: before your confession I knew there were many shameful things that people said you were guilty of; this grieved me very much, both because of the offence given to God and because of your own reputation, which I was at a loss how to defend; but now I am able to answer everything that may be said against you." "But, my Father, the past will always be true." "No," he replied, "for if people judge you as the Pharisees judged St. Magdalen, you will have our Lord Himself and your own conscience to defend you." "But you yourself, my Father, what do you think of the past?" "Nothing, I assure you; for how could you expect my thoughts to dwell upon that which no longer exists in the sight of God? How shall I think of nothing except not to think at all. I shall think only of praising the Lord and of celebrating the feast of your conversion. Yes, I desire to celebrate it in union with the angels of heaven who rejoice over your change of heart." And as he said these things tears trickled down from his eyes. "You are weeping, no doubt," said the penitent, "over the abomination of my life." "Oh no," replied the holy prelate, "I am weeping with joy over your resurrection to the life of grace." (*The Spirit of St. Francis de Sales*, pp. 134–135)

Pause: Consider the last time you cried. How would Jesus empathize and commiserate with you?

Francis's Words

Gentleness, as a little virtue that Francis so ably demonstrated to others, begins first of all with our attitude toward ourselves, particularly as our spiritual journey requires much effort.

> One of the best exercises in meekness we can perform is when the subject is in ourselves. We must not fret over our own imperfections. Although reason requires that we must be displeased and sorry whenever we commit a fault, we must refrain from bitter, gloomy, spiteful, and emotional displeasure. Many people are greatly at fault in this way. When overcome by anger they become angry at being angry, disturbed at being disturbed, and vexed at being vexed. By such means they keep their hearts drenched and steeped in passion.
>
> . . . A father's gentle, loving rebuke has far greater power to correct a child than rage and passion. So too when we have committed some fault if we rebuke our heart by a calm, mild remonstrance, with more compassion for it than passion against it and encourage it to make amendment, then repentance conceived in this way will sink far deeper and penetrate more effectually than fretful, angry, stormy repentance. (*Introduction to the Devout Life*, pp. 149–150)

When this gentleness sinks deep within us, it wells up again to become a stream of good will for serving others.

> Don't lose any opportunity, however small, of being gentle toward everyone. Don't rely on your own efforts to succeed in your various undertakings, but only on God's help. Then rest in His care of you, confident that He will do what is best for you, provided that you, for your part, work diligently but gently. I say "gently" because a tense diligence is harmful both to our heart and to our task and is not really diligence, but rather overeagerness and anxiety. (*Letters of Spiritual Direction*, p. 159)

Do not worry yourself; no, believe me, practice serving our Lord with a gentleness full of strength and zeal. That is the true method of this service. Wish not to do all, but only something, and without doubt you will do much. (*Thy Will Be Done*, p. 153)

Reflection

Gentleness, meekness, civility, sweetness—all are notions bound up in the distinctively Salesian virtue of *douceur*.

> *Douceur* is a quality of person that corresponds to the light burden offered by the Matthean Jesus to those otherwise heavy-laden. It connotes an almost maternal quality of serving that is swathed in tender concern. Salesian *douceur* also suggests a sense of being grace-filled, graceful in the broadest use of the term. This gracefulness extends from external demeanor—polite manners and convivial disposition—to the very quality of a person's heart—the way in which a person is interiorly ordered and disposed. (*Letters of Spiritual Direction*, p. 64)

This ordering and disposition of the heart flows naturally from humility, and together with it forms the dual framework for the Salesian life of devotion. Like humility, gentleness is also a virtue to be cultivated in all the ordinary affairs of our life, so as to reproduce the image of Jesus walking again in our midst.

✧ Prayerfully read the account of the woman caught in adultery (John 8:1–11). Imagine yourself standing in the woman's shoes.
✦ What occasions do others have for bringing charges against you? What charges would you bring against yourself?
✦ Look at Jesus as he writes on the ground in front of you. What is he thinking? What would you say to him?
✦ Repeat over and over the words of Jesus, now spoken to you: "Neither do I condemn you. Go your way, and from now on do not sin again." Give thanks to God for the gentleness shown to you.

✧ Examine how "graceful" you are in social situations. Are you genuinely polite to those whom you meet, even to strangers? Do you find yourself avoiding anyone? How could you better show concern for those who come to you for help?

✧ Consider the people with whom you work. Are you unnecessarily critical of their faults? Do you treat them with loving persuasion or commanding force? How could you be more gentle to those who are a "heavy burden" to you?

✧ Francis de Sales wrote in a letter to a married woman, "Take care to bring contentment to him to whom God has espoused you; like a honeybee, while you are carefully making the honey of devotion, at the same time make the wax of your household affairs" (*Letters of Spiritual Direction*, p. 167). Using this image, reflect on your ability to make both "honey" and "wax" at the same time, either in your family or within your community.

✧ Stand before a crucifix. Imagine yourself as one of the few people remaining there before Jesus. See the look that he gives you. Feel the gentle compassion in his heart. Hear him say, "'Father, forgive them; for they do not know what they are doing'" (Luke 23:34). Make this your own thought and apply it gently to those who wrong you this day.

God's Word

At that time Jesus said, "I thank you, Father, Lord of heaven and earth, because you have hidden these things from the wise and the intelligent and have revealed them to infants; yes, Father, for such was your gracious will. All things have been handed over to me by my Father; and no one knows the Son except the Father, and no one knows the Father except the Son and anyone to whom the Son chooses to reveal him.

"Come to me, all you that are weary and are carrying heavy burdens, and I will give you rest. Take my yoke upon you, and learn from me; for I am gentle and humble in heart, and you will find rest for your souls. For my yoke is easy, and my burden is light." (Matthew 11:25–30)

Closing prayer:

Gentle God, help us to keep our eyes lifted up on high to you; increase our courage by holy humility, fortify it with meekness, confirm it by a steady effort. Give us the grace to make our minds rule over our inclinations and moods and not to allow fears to take hold of our heart. May the efforts we make this day teach us how to be gentle each day that follows.

✧ **Meditation 12** ✧

Entrusting Our Lowly Lives

Theme: "God allows many difficulties to beset those who want to serve him but he never lets them sink beneath the burden as long as they trust in him" (*Selected Letters*, p. 246).

Opening prayer: Dear God, help us to see our own powerlessness as the seat of your omnipotence and our misery as the throne of your mercy. May we entrust our lowly lives to you that your glory be made known to all.

About Francis

Beyond the little virtues practiced along the way of devotion, Francis demonstrated the continual desire to mortify his self-centeredness so as to be ever more filled with the love of God. He was able to practice this holy abandonment or detachment in a particular way as he dealt with suffering.

Francis was often plagued with sickness. During his student days at Padua, he was stricken with a severe fever, accompanied "by a troublesome dysentery."

On January 15, 1591, the doctors judged Francis lost, and Déage [his tutor] was delegated to inform him of his approaching death. Francis received the news "with courage and joy." Déage ventured to ask him: "Where do you wish to be buried? What funeral arrangements do you

89

want carried out?" "I see I have only a spiritual testament to make: that I give back my soul to God. As for my body, when I am dead, give it, I pray you, to the medical students so that—having been of no use to the world during my life—it may be useful for something after my death." (Ravier, *Sage and Saint*, p. 41)

This bout with illness would be the first of a lifelong series of physical problems for Francis. As Jane de Chantal remarked:

I very often saw him ill or else heard him mention a variety of ailments, for instance fevers, quinsy [i.e., angina], gastric and abdominal inflammations and sickness, which weakened him considerably and sapped his strength; besides this, there was the continual distress caused by haemorrhoids of many years' standing. In his last years all his infirmities got very much worse: he had violent headaches and abdominal and kidney pains, painful and weak legs with unhealed sores. He was so terribly exhausted that it filled one's heart with pity to watch him walking. There were other things which people knew nothing about and which he hid as much as he could, not changing his life, his manner or the expression on his face. The only way you could tell he was feeling ill was by his colour, for he never took to his bed except for really drastic illness. (Stopp, ed., *A Testimony by St. Chantal*, p. 94)

Nevertheless, as one of his doctors testifies, Francis never grew impatient or complained; he readily submitted to every treatment that was prescribed for him, including several bleedings, without speaking a word or even clenching his teeth!

Pause: Consider your own physical condition. How do you deal with pain and sickness?

Francis's Words

Detachment, for Francis, was a matter of stepping back from one's own desires and plans so as to step forward and "take up the cross" of God's will as it is manifested in the conditions of our life.

"To take up your cross . . . is to receive and suffer with entire submission all the pains, contradictions, afflictions and mortifications that come to you in life, be they little or great, agreeable or repugnant to your tastes, in a word all without exception. We would like very much to choose our crosses, to have a different one from that which we carry, or perhaps to carry a heavy one to which a little glory is attached rather than a light one that is more obscure but fatigues us by its persistence. This is an illusion! We must carry the cross we have and not another, and its merit does not consist in the quality of the cross but in the perfection with which it is carried." (*The Spirit of St. Francis de Sales*, pp. 230–231)

To carry the cross of our suffering, Francis encouraged a simple method for offering one's heart to the Savior:

First, accept the pain from His hand, as if you saw Him Himself putting and pressing it on your head.

Second, offer yourself to suffer more.

Third, beg our Savior by the merit of His torments to accept these little distresses in union with the pains He suffered on the Cross.

Next, protest that you wish not only to suffer, but to love and cherish these sufferings since they are sent from so good and so sweet a hand.

Lastly, invoke the martyrs and the many servants of God, who enjoy Heaven as a result of their having been afflicted in this world. (*Thy Will Be Done*, p. 100)

Even beyond the particular pains that accompany an illness, Francis would have us be detached, abandoned, and resigned with regard to all the plans we make for our life.

We will soon be in eternity, and then we will see how . . . little it matters whether they [the affairs of this world] turn out or not. At this time, nevertheless, we apply ourselves to them as if they were great things. When we were little children, with what eagerness did we put together little bits of tile, wood, and mud, to make houses and small buildings! And if someone destroyed them, we were very grieved and tearful at it; but now we know well that it all mattered very little. One day it will be the same with us in Heaven, when we will see that our concerns in this world were truly only child's play. (*Thy Will Be Done*, p. 48)

Reflection

All too often pleasure is sought after as the means to, or the equivalent of, happiness. In this view, any pain associated with suffering is viewed as something to be avoided at all costs. For Christians, though, "take up your cross" remains a rallying cry for the spiritual life.

In the Salesian tradition, the crosses we must bear are not only times of persecution or suffering that happen despite our wishes. Rather, they are all the events of our daily life in which the contrast between our own will and that of God is displayed. These include those little things that annoy us by the fact that they happen continually, and those things that befall us through no fault of our own. And so, by learning to let go of our own desire not to suffer, and to let God's will be paramount in our life, we will be better able to travel the spiritual journey in peace.

✧ Make a list of the little crosses that you encounter in your everyday routine. What is it that makes them seem unbearable? How could you carry them better? How might these little annoyances be transformed into opportunities for experiencing God's grace and demonstrating your love?

✧ Examine your own capacity to carry the cross of suffering as prescribed by Francis in the previous "Francis's Words" section.

✦ Are you able to accept pain when you are not able to prevent it?

✦ How does your pain compare with that which Jesus suffered on the cross?

✦ Can you offer yourself to suffer more, if it is God's will to benefit you in this way?

✧ Picture in your mind the stark reality of Jesus suffering on the cross. Listen again to his words from the cross and reflect upon his total abandonment to the will of God:

+ "'Father, forgive them; for they do not know what they are doing'" (Luke 23:34). Can you let go of the hurts you have suffered at the hands of someone close to you? Will you let God forgive them, too?
+ "'Truly I tell you, today you will be with me in paradise'" (Luke 23:43). Can you let go of your desires for a better life now? Will you let God provide for you as God sees fit?
+ "When Jesus saw his mother and the disciple whom he loved standing beside her, he said to his mother, 'Woman, here is your son.' Then he said to the disciple, 'Here is your mother'" (John 19:26–27). Can you let go of others as their relationship to you changes? Will you let God lead you in caring for others?
+ "'My God, my God, why have you forsaken me?'" (Mark 15:34). Can you let go of seeking the consolations of prayer so as to embrace the God to whom you pray? Will you let God be God and not try to conform the divine will to your own?
+ "'I am thirsty'" (John 19:28). Can you let go of some addiction or other need that controls you? Will you let God provide for you through the generosity of others?
+ "'It is finished'" (John 19:30). Can you let go of the works that have taken so much of your time? Will you let God lead you elsewhere without resistance?
+ "'Father, into your hands I commend my spirit'" (Luke 23:46). Can you let go of your own self-will? Will you let God be the sole provider for your life?

✧ As a reflective exercise, draw, sculpt, or carve a cross. Decorate it with "jewels" that represent what you pray for, what you most desire in your life now. Do you want success or good health or material things? Do you seek courage or understanding or wisdom? Do you pray for detachment or simply that God's will may be done? Be honest in your depiction. Mark down the date and plan to review this prayer and contemplate the message of this cross four months from now.

✧ Read a selection from a Lives of the Saints, particularly the examples of the martyrs. How do the events of your life compare with theirs, especially those that involve suffering? How might you be able to become a saint today through your own experiences of detachment and abandonment to the will of God? Choose one example from these holy lives and set out to imitate it in your own. Compose a prayer that honors this saint. Write it out and place it on your mirror or in a regularly used prayer book.

God's Word

Let each of you look not to your own interests, but to the interests of others. Let the same mind be in you that was in Christ Jesus,
>who, though he was in the form of God,
>>did not regard equality with God
>>as something to be exploited,
>but emptied himself,
>>taking the form of a slave,
>>being born in human likeness.
>And being found in human form,
>>he humbled himself
>>and became obedient to the point of death—
>>even death on a cross.

>Therefore God also highly exalted him
>>and gave him the name
>>that is above every name,
>so that at the name of Jesus
>>every knee should bend,
>>in heaven and on earth and under the earth,
>and every tongue should confess
>>that Jesus is Lord,
>>to the glory of God.

(Philippians 2:4–11)

Closing prayer:

Live, Jesus, live, your death upon the tree;
Shows all your boundless love for me!

Lord, give us the grace to die to all other loves in order to live in your love, so that we may not die eternally. (Adapted from *Treatise on the Love of God*, vol. 2, p. 281)

✧ Meditation 13 ✧

Have No Fear!

Theme: "Avoid anxiety and worries, for nothing so impedes our progress toward perfection" (*Letters of Spiritual Direction*, p. 125).

Opening prayer: Dear God, may the greatness of our hope in eternal life keep beneath our notice all the anxious affairs of our life on earth.

About Francis

Beyond the physical distress which he suffered, Francis often encountered situations in which his life was at peril. Nevertheless, his mission of fulfilling the will of God in ministering to others took precedence over his own safety.

> One day when he was riding in a frail bark on the lake of Geneva, he seemed to experience ineffable joy because his life was completely in the hands of Providence since only a thin little board separated him from death; and when he was asked how he could preserve such equanimity of soul he replied: "When one's confidence is placed in the unchangeable God, one cannot possibly change; this confidence is the immutable pole around which all my actions and desires revolve." (P. 45)

This fearlessness also showed itself in dealing with precarious people:

> "How is it," he was asked one day, "that you expose yourself to danger so often from the hands of heretics?" "It is not from boldness," he replied, "nor from simplicity of soul, but from entire confidence in the Providence of God. Must we not leave our life and all we are at the disposition of this adorable Providence? For we are no longer our own but His Who to render us His own has wished in so loving a manner to be entirely ours." (*The Spirit of St. Francis de Sales*, pp. 45–46)

Pause: Consider your present situation at home or at work. What is your greatest worry?

Francis's Words

In Francis's understanding of life, "with the single exception of sin, anxiety is the greatest evil that can happen [to us]" (*Introduction to the Devout Life*, p. 251). This is why optimism is so essential for the spiritual journey.

Francis believed that when we preserve this confident virtue, any calamities that might befall us along the way lose their destructive power.

> "Let us leave all that to Providence. . . . God knows better than we what we need and provided we keep his commandments He will turn all things to our good. We must try to preserve an evenness of temper amid so great an unevenness of events, and though all things around us change we must strive to remain unchanged, with our eyes fixed on God above. Let everything be topsy-turvy, not only without us but even within; let our heart be sad or joyful, in sweetness or bitterness, in peace or in trouble, in light or darkness, in temptations or at rest; let the sun scorch us or the dew refresh, it matters not, our will must ever be directed to the good pleasure of God, our only and sovereign Good. This is the target of perfection at

which we all must aim; and he who comes nearest gets the prize." (*The Spirit of St. Francis de Sales*, p. 63)

Thus, it is optimism that enables us to confide the events of our life to the good pleasure of God's will, just as simple children humbly trust in the gently loving guidance of their parents.

> As long as you realize that God is holding on to you by your will and resolution to serve him, go on boldly and do not be upset by your little set-backs and falls; there is no need to be put out by this provided you throw yourself into his arms from time to time and kiss him with the kiss of charity. Go on joyfully and with your heart as open and widely trustful as possible; and if you cannot always be joyful, at least be brave and confident. (*Selected Letters*, pp. 45–46)

> Go straight on, and always in God's sight. God takes pleasure in seeing you make your little steps; and like a good father who holds his child by the hand, he will conform his steps to yours and will be quite happy not to go any faster than you. What are you anxious about? Whether you are taking this road or that other way, going fast or slow? All that matters is that he is with you, and you with him. (*Selected Letters*, p. 160)

Reflection

The virtue of optimism, for Francis, stems from his fundamental conviction that the God who created us continues to love us, notwithstanding our imperfections. In Francis's view, the excellence of God's grace is always greater than any temptation we face or sin we commit.

There is reason, then, never to be afraid, but always to be hopeful. Because of the providential care that God holds out to us, we can actively and energetically cast aside our anxieties and worries, knowing that "neither death, nor life, nor angels, nor rulers, nor things present, nor things to come, nor powers, nor height, nor depth, nor anything else in all creation, will be able to separate us from the love of God in Christ Jesus" (Romans 8:38–39).

✧ Read prayerfully the observations of Jesus in Matthew 6:25–34 with regard to life cycles among plants and birds. Listen closely as he poses his questions directly to you.

✦ Is not life more than the food you worry about, and the body more than the clothing that you shop for?

✦ Are you not of more value than the birds of the air who do nothing productive but are fed nonetheless?

✦ Can you, by worrying, add a single hour to your span of life?

✦ Admitting the obvious answers, entrust your anxieties to God's providence.

✧ Consider the stark reality that awaits us all: imagine yourself on your death bed with no hope of recovery. What is it that makes this close encounter so dreadful? What would be your greatest fear? Cast your anxious feelings upon God, knowing that God awaits you with arms open to embrace you for all eternity.

✧ Conduct a general examination of your life to this point. Make a "top ten" list of the best things that have happened to you. Make another list of the worst things. Which list is more significant to you? Where is God to be found in both lists? Which things would you change if you could? Ask for God's grace to keep in mind the best and to cast away the fear of the worst.

✧ Take in hand a flower with many petals. Imagine for each of the petals one cause of anxiety that you have right now. Pluck one petal at a time and ponder the worrisome thing that it represents. Then toss each one to heaven, praying that God will take away the worry as the wind blows away the petal.

✧ Take a baby or a toddler for a walk. Carry the baby in your arms, or hold the toddler by the hand. As you are enjoying this small person, the being-together, and the out-of-doors, be aware of the security and dependability you are providing in this experience. If you are walking together, notice how you do (or do not!) pace yourself according to the child's capabilities. When you have quiet, private time at the end of the day, reread "Francis's Words," settling your affections on a God who has begotten you and moves with you on your life's journey.

God's Word

Pondering the powerful hand of God, be humble so that God may exalt you in time. Give any fears over to God because your loving Creator cares for you. The evil one roars like a lion and hunts for prey. Hold fast, defend yourself with your faith. Your sisters and brothers undergo similar suffering. Fear not because the suffering will end, and God will grace you with strength, healing, and support. All power and glory to God, now and forever. Amen. (Adapted from 1 Peter 5:6–11)

Closing prayer: "O God, you are my God, and I will put my trust in you; you will stand by me and be my refuge, and I shall fear nothing, for not only are you with me, but you are in me and I am in you" (*Selected Letters*, p. 262).

✧ Meditation 14 ✧

Ask for Nothing, Refuse Nothing

Theme: "We must neither ask anything or refuse anything, but leave ourselves absolutely in the arms of divine Providence, without busying ourselves with any desires, except to will what God wills of us" (*Spiritual Conferences*, p. 400).

Opening prayer:

Dear God, make our hearts like a ball of wax in your hands, ready to receive all the impressions of your eternal good pleasure. Make us equally ready for all things, and help us to have no other object for our delight except your will. (Adapted from *Treatise on the Love of God*, vol. 2, pp. 106–107)

About Francis

Francis had a deep yearning to love God in all things and above all things. And, of the many events that took place in his life, perhaps none so aptly demonstrates this desire as the crisis that captivated him as a young student.

While studying in Paris, Francis came to be perplexed by what he learned about the ways of God. On the one hand, he listened with wondrous enthusiasm to lectures on the Canticle of Canticles, that great love poetry of the Hebrew Scriptures. Reading this poetry as symbolic of the love between God and the human heart, Francis was deeply moved by the revelation of the lyrics, so much so that afterward "he was no longer able to conceive of the spiritual life except as a love story, the most beautiful of love stories" (Ravier, *Sage and Saint*, p. 31).

On the other hand, Francis also heard the ongoing debate among theologians concerning the matter of predestination. Pondering the possibility that some persons are destined for eternal damnation, he wondered whether he, in fact, was one of their number. Soon he became convinced that he was, and the thought of his own misery enveloped him in great anguish. His desire to be united with God, it seemed, was not to be realized.

Kneeling one day in the chapel of the Virgin Mary, Francis made "an act of heroic abandonment" and prayed thus:

> Whatever you have decided, Lord, in the eternal decree of your predestination, and of your retribution, you whose judgments are an immense abyss . . . , I shall love you, Lord, in this life at least, if it is not granted me to love you in the eternal life. (Ravier, *Sage and Saint*, p. 32)

Afterward Francis found that his temptation to despair vanished; his heart was once again at peace. Later, when the young student became the master teacher, the attainment of a holy indifference to the will of God would become the high point of his spirituality.

Pause: Consider your future. What is the one thing you desire most for your life?

Francis's Words

Because union with God is the final goal of the spiritual journey, Francis believed that all other desires were ultimately to be renounced—even the desire for God. He sought to entrust himself entirely to the providence of God. He expressed this goal with a favorite image:

"Remain simply where God puts you . . . and just as he places you there like a statue in a niche, animated with this sentiment that we belong entirely to God and that God is all ours; this is the way we must love. If a statue in a niche could speak and some one were to ask: 'Why are you there?' it would simply answer: 'Because my master has put me here.' 'Why do you not move from where you are?' 'Because he wants me to stay where I am.' 'What will it benefit you to remain there?' 'That is not for me to judge; I have simply to obey the will of my master.' 'But you do not see him?' 'No, but he sees me and is pleased that I am here where he put me.' 'But would you not prefer to move so as to be nearer to him?' 'No, at least not till he commands me to do so.' 'Do you then desire nothing?' 'No, for the good pleasure of my master is the sole desire of my heart.'" (*The Spirit of St. Francis de Sales*, p. 62)

In what would become his farewell address to the sisters of the Visitation, he offers an autobiographical reflection on the subject:

I wish for few things; what I do desire, I desire for God; I have scarcely any desires, but were I to begin life again, I would have, or would wish to have, none at all. If God came to me, favouring me with the sensible feeling of His presence, I also would go to Him, accepting His grace and corresponding therewith; but if He did not choose to come to me, I would stay where I was, and would not move towards Him. What I mean is that I would not strive after the feeling of His presence, but would content myself with apprehending Him by faith alone. (*Spiritual Conferences*, p. 399)

Reflection

Francis was keen on planning for holiness by seeking out how best to serve God in the ordinary events of his daily life. Nevertheless, above and beyond the preparation of the day, Francis counseled a complete detachment from and optimistic abandonment to the Divine Will. In the spiritual life, the only plan we need to follow is God's plan!

For Francis, what divine providence has in store for us can only be good, as the God who loves us will certainly give us the grace to follow where God leads us. When it becomes difficult to embrace or even accept the many things that happen to us, because they are variations from our own plan of life, then is the time to practice holy indifference. As we learn to do this, we will find the inner peace and tranquillity of spirit that allows us to love God above all things and to be united with God in all things.

✧ Read again Francis's imaginary dialog about the statue in the niche and answer the questions as if they were posed to you.

✧ Prayerfully read the beginning of Jesus' last discourse in John 14:1–7 and reflect on your own "holy indifference":
✦ Is your heart troubled by the fear of the future? What role does your own faith play in this?
✦ What "dwelling place" do you imagine that God has prepared for you?
✦ Do you really know Jesus? How is he "the way, and the truth, and the life" for you?

✧ Imagine that you could begin your life over again. What would you change? What would you wish for yourself? How can you begin anew this very day?

✧ Consider making your own farewell statements to those whom you love.
✦ If you could create a spiritual version of your last will and testament, what would you leave and to whom? Would you leave anything you have received from God to others?
✦ If you could write your own epitaph, to be inscribed on your headstone for all to see and read, what would it say? What would you like most to be remembered for?

✧ Take a small ball of wax and put it on your dresser. In the morning, as your prepare for your day, take the wax in hand and pray again the opening prayer of this meditation. Keep the ball with you during the day to remind you of this prayer and of the transforming action of God's grace as it shapes your life.

God's Word

Upon my bed at night
    I sought him whom my soul loves;
I sought him, but found him not;
    I called him, but he gave no answer.
"I will rise now and go about the city,
    in the streets and in the squares;
I will seek him whom my soul loves."
    I sought him, but found him not.
The sentinels found me,
    as they went about in the city.
"Have you seen him whom my soul loves?"
Scarcely had I passed them,
    when I found him whom my soul loves.
I held him, and would not let him go.

(Song of Solomon 3:1–4)

Closing prayer:

Divine Lover, looking upon your infant Son, we see how your tender mercy provides for our eternal needs. Give us the grace to desire nothing and to refuse nothing, but, as Jesus did, to suffer and to receive with perfect evenness of mind all that your providence may permit.

✧ Meditation 15 ✧

The Beauty of Creation

Theme: Seeing the beauty of the world around us leads us little by little to finding God within us, for God "'as sovereign beauty is author of the beauteous harmony, beauteous luster, and good grace in all things'" (*Treatise on the Love of God*, vol. 1, p. 54).

Opening prayer: My great and good Creator, how great is my debt to you since you were moved to draw me out of nothing and by your mercy to make me what I am!

About Francis

In October of 1621, the last year of his life, Francis envisioned for himself an apostolic retreat to the hermitage of Saint-Germain, high up in the mountains near the lake of Annecy. There he would be able to witness firsthand the beauty of creation, as he "contemplated at length the admirable panorama of mountains capped with their first snow, of forests already gilded by autumn, and the blue lake, at the end of which one perceived the roofs of the suburbs of Annecy" (Ravier, *Sage and Saint*, p. 241). There, too, Francis would give expression to an ardent desire of his soul:

"It is decided," he said. "Since I have a coadjutor, if it can be arranged by the will of some princes, I shall come up

107

here! This is where I must have my retreat. I shall live in this hermitage because I have chosen it. . . . O God! What a good and pleasant thing for us to be here! Yes, definitely, I must leave to our coadjutor the burden and heat of the day, while with our Rosary and our pen we shall serve God and his Church here!" (Ravier, *Sage and Saint*, p. 242)

Dreaming thus of one day retiring from the duties of the pastoral office that he held, Francis rejoiced in the possibility of a new and renewed lifestyle. Yet his words are far from being wistful ruminations. They reveal not so much a desire to get away from it all as a longing to be immersed in the very heart of it all, there where the splendor of the natural world shone forth for all to see.

Pause: Consider your own favorite "island" and rest a moment there in its peacefulness.

Francis's Words

For Francis, beholding the beauty of the world is a salutary means of drawing closer to union with God, who is both the source and final end of all creation. The recognition of the interdependence of all creatures led Francis to prayerful delight:

Ah, if a man would consider this general commerce and traffic which creatures have with one another in such perfect correspondence, with how many amorous passions for this sovereign wisdom would he be moved, so that he would cry out, "Your providence, O Father great and eternal, governs all things!" (*Treatise on the Love of God*, vol. 1, p. 109)

From this principle of God's providential goodness, Francis derived his teaching that the Incarnation of Jesus was intended by God from the very beginning of creation as its apex:

From among all the creatures that God's supreme omnipotence could bring into being, he thought it good to choose that humanity which later was actually united to the person of God the Son. For it he destined the incomparable dignity of personal union with his divine majesty, so that it might eternally and pre-eminently enjoy the treasures of his infinite glory.

And to this perfect creation would be joined all other humans, as sharers in the beauty of God.

After choosing for this happy state the sacred humanity of our Savior, supreme providence then decreed that he would not restrict his bounty solely to the person of his beloved Son, but for that Son's sake he would diffuse it among many other creatures. Out of the sum of the countless number of beings he could produce he chose to create men and angels to have company with his Son, to participate in his grace and glory, and to adore and praise him forevermore. (*Treatise on the Love of God*, vol. 1, pp. 111–112)

Thus, for Francis, we are drawn to participate in this cosmic dance of divine love by an appreciative awareness of the beauty that surrounds us.

Reflection

Inspired by his cultural surroundings, Francis exalts the Christian aesthetic to a place of prominence along the spiritual journey in this thought:

All that is beautiful, harmonious, good, and graceful in the world participates in God by virtue of those qualities. The contemplation of beauty, then, for the humanist tradition that Francis became acquainted with at Padua, can lead to the contemplation of God. Salesian spirituality is marked in its celebration of whatever in the created order participates in the beauty evocative of God. (*Letters of Spiritual Direction*, p. 36)

So, what was in the beginning, from God's point of view—the goodness of creation—is now the end and aim of our spiritual journey, namely, union with the creator God in the divine milieu that is the perfection of the universe. To reach this end, we go back again and again to the beginning of prayer, to celebrate the beauteous presence of our God that is around us and within us.

✧ Read prayerfully the first story of creation in Genesis, chapter 1, and reflect on the beauty that constitutes the "good" of each day:

✦ Allow yourself to bask in the light of sunrise or sunset.
✦ Ponder the vastness of the sky and the universal presence of God.
✦ Appreciate the gift of the earth and consider what you might do for a better ecosystem.
✦ Consider the power of time and the limitation that it imposes on us as a reminder of our creatureliness.
✦ Marvel at the wonders of the animal world and see in the birds and fishes the hand of the good Creator.
✦ Think about our human life as intimately connected with all other living things, and give thanks to God.

✧ Make an examination of the beauty of your own life. List the "top ten" good qualities of your character.

✦ How are these gifts of the Creator?
✦ How have you endeavored to develop them further?
✦ How are these beautiful traits noticeable to others?

✧ Visit a local park. Sit there in the midst of creation and be still. What do you see around you that is beautiful and why is it so? How can you see God in that beauty?

✧ Read prayerfully the final vision of the Bible in Revelation 21:1–7 and imagine a world of perfect beauty.

✦ What do you imagine "a new heaven and a new earth" will be like?
✦ How do you picture the "new Jerusalem" in terms of the dwelling place that is your own surroundings, your workplace, or your family?
✦ What is the "spring of the water of life" that gives you refreshment? How does prayer provide life-giving water to you?

God's Word

How I love your dwelling place,
Yahweh Sabaoth!
How my soul yearns and pines for your courts!
My heart and my flesh cry out to you, the living God.
Finally, the sparrow has found its home,
the swallow a nest for its young—
your altars, Yahweh Sabaoth, O my God.
Happy those who dwell in your house
and praise you all day long.

(Psalm 84:1–4)

Closing prayer:

God, Creator of the universe, we offer you thanks and praise. Among the beauties of your creation, you have given us the capability of eternal life. May we be perfectly united to your divine majesty when you bring this world to its completion.

DEVOTION

✧ For Further Reading ✧

Original Writings of Saint Francis de Sales

Introduction to the Devout Life. Translated by John K. Ryan. Garden City, NY: Doubleday and Company, Image Books, 1972.

Francis de Sales, Jane de Chantal: Letters of Spiritual Direction. Translated by Péronne Marie Thibert. Selected and introduced by Wendy M. Wright and Joseph F. Power. Mahwah, NJ: Paulist Press, 1988.

The Mystical Exposition of the Canticle of Canticles. Translated, with notes, by Thomas F. Dailey. Center Valley, PA: Allentown College, 1996.

Spiritual Directory of St. Francis de Sales: Reflections for the Laity. Compiled by Lewis S. Fiorelli. Boston: Daughters of Saint Paul, 1985.

Spiritual Exercises. Translated by William N. Doughtery. Edited with an introductory essay, notes, and a bio-bibliographical note by Joseph F. Chorpenning. Toronto: Peregrina Publishing Company, 1993.

Thy Will Be Done: Letters to Persons in the World. Manchester, NH: Sophia Institute Press, 1995.

Treatise on the Love of God (2 volumes). Translated by John K. Ryan. Rockford, IL: Tan Books and Publishers, 1974–75.

Edited Collections

Daily Readings with St. Francis de Sales. Edited by Michael Hollings. Springfield, IL: Templegate Publishers, 1985.

Francis de Sales: Finding God Wherever You Are. Selected spiritual writings, introduced and edited by Joseph F. Power. New Rochelle, NY: New York City Press, 1993.

Francis de Sales: Introduction to the Devout Life and Treatise on the Love of God. Edited and introduced by Wendy M. Wright. New York: Crossroad, 1993.

Biographical Studies

Ravier, André. *Francis de Sales: Sage and Saint.* Translated by Joseph D. Bowler. San Francisco: Ignatius Press, 1988.

Wright, Wendy M. *Bond of Perfection: Jeanne de Chantal and François de Sales.* New York: Paulist Press, 1985.

Acknowledgments *(continued)*

The psalms in this book are from *Psalms Anew: In Inclusive Language,* compiled by Nancy Schreck and Maureen Leach (Winona, MN: Saint Mary's Press, 1986). Copyright © 1986 by Saint Mary's Press. All rights reserved.

All other scriptural quotations in this book are from the New Revised Standard Version of the Bible. Copyright © 1989 by the Division of Christian Education of the National Council of the Churches of Christ in the United States of America. All rights reserved.

The excerpts on pages 14–15, 16, 17, 28, 38, 39, 43, 60, 89–90, 103, 103, 107, and 107–108 are from *Francis de Sales: Sage and Saint,* by André Ravier, SJ, translated by Joseph D. Bowler, OSFS (San Francisco: Ignatius Press, 1988), pages 20, 62, 85, 137, 50, 50–51, 120, 137, 41, 31, 32, 241, and 242, respectively. Copyright © 1988 by Ignatius Press. Used by permission.

The excerpts on pages 19, 40, 45, 49, 57, 76–77, 89, 98, 98, and 101 are from *Selected Letters,* by Francis de Sales, translated by Elisabeth Stopp (New York: Harper and Brothers, 1960), pages 33–34, 191, 158, 162, 21, 157, 246, 45–46, 160, and 262, respectively. Copyright © 1960 by Elisabeth Stopp.

The excerpts on pages 20, 26, 27, 28, 43, 59, 61, 61, 61–62, 67, 70, 71–72, 75, 78, 85, and 97 are from *Introduction to the Devout Life,* by Francis de Sales, translated by John K. Ryan (Garden City, NY: Doubleday and Company, Image Books, 1972), pages 33–34, 184, 121–122, 184, 102, 174, 176–177, 169–170, 174–175, 127–128, 128, 129 and 130, 128, 139, 149–150, and 251, respectively. Copyright © 1950 by Harper and Brothers, © 1966 by John K. Ryan. Used by permission of Doubleday, a division of Bantam Doubleday Dell Publishing Group.

The excerpt by Francis de Sales on page 24 is from *On the Preacher and Preaching,* translated by John K. Ryan (N.p.: Henry Regnery Company, 1964), page 50. Copyright © 1964 by Henry Regnery Company.

Titles in the Companions for the Journey Series

Praying with Anthony of Padua

Praying with Benedict

Praying with Catherine McAuley

Praying with Catherine of Siena

Praying with Clare of Assisi

Praying with Dominic

Praying with Dorothy Day

Praying with Elizabeth Seton

Praying with Francis de Sales

Praying with Francis of Assisi

Praying with Hildegard of Bingen

Praying with Ignatius of Loyola

Praying with John Baptist de La Salle

Praying with John Cardinal Newman

Praying with John of the Cross

Praying with Julian of Norwich

Praying with Louise de Marillac

Praying with Teresa of Ávila

Praying with Thérèse of Lisieux

Praying with Thomas Merton

Praying with Vincent de Paul

Order from your local religious bookstore or from

Saint Mary's Press
702 TERRACE HEIGHTS
WINONA, MN 55987-1320
USA
1-800-533-8095